Praise for

From Athletics to Engineering: 8 Ways to Support Diversity, Equity, and Inclusion for All

"I absolutely love the book. It is as well organized, written, researched and humanistically authored as any book I have read or listened to. I believe this book should be required reading for every school and college in America, every sports team, every police department (which you both support and call for change), and every corporation."

Gino Blefari, CEO, HomeServices of America, Inc. and Chairman, Berkshire Hathaway HomeServices Worldwide, Minneapolis, Minnesota, USA

"I have been searching for a book on diversity that would offer some commonsense guidance on how to do my part. This is the book I have been seeking! Michael and Johnnie have extended an inspiring and heartfelt invitation to all of us to roll up our sleeves and join them in learning how to put in the effort needed to make our world a more inclusive, supportive, and loving place. I think this book is especially useful for teachers like me and recommend it for anyone looking to be an active partner in this space."

Alison Schnettler, preschool teacher, Louisville, Colorado, USA

"Johnnie and Michael deliver a book that goes beyond platitudes. Each chapter is jam-packed with actionable strategies that managers can use to create a more diverse, equitable, and inclusive workplace. Read it. Read it again. And then read it with your team."

Daron K. Roberts, author of *Call an Audible* and Director, Center for Sports Leadership & Innovation, The University of Texas at Austin, Austin, Texas, USA

"As a science teacher and someone who loves sports, I found the analogies in the book were a match made in heaven. The book was well organized, and the steps were carefully laid out so that even individuals as young as 15 would be able to understand the message the book was trying to convey. I found many of the stories relatable, powerful, and inspirational."

Rebecca Reyna Neal, Chemistry and Physics Teacher, Three Rivers Jr/Sr High School, Three Rivers, Texas, USA

"This book is incredibly relevant for the times. Johnnie and Michael were honest, tactful, and most importantly, empathetic in sharing why diversity and inclusion efforts are so important in the world today."

**Eric Impraim, Insurance Marketing Portfolio
Manager, Tucson, Arizona, USA**

Finally! A book that puts forth steps we can take to solve biases and prejudices. The 8 Ways they recommend are powerful, each and every one. This book will become dinged up, dog-eared and post-it-noted on my desk as I put it to use EVERY DAY in my own journey to temper bias and stay focused on getting to the goal together.

**Bobbi Burke, Owner/Broker/REALTOR®, Envoy Real
Estate Services, LLC, Phoenix Arizona, USA**

8 Ways is an outstandingly well-written book and provides a simple and practical roadmap—a game plan—designed to support DEI in the workplace and in day-to-day life. Today, DEI is a fearful topic because, while society has a general sense of what a successful DEI implementation feels like, we previously did not have a specific game plan of how to get there. Now we do!

**John Tortora, Attorney, Former President of the San Jose Sharks and
National Hockey League Executive, Morgan Hill, California, USA**

FROM ATHLETICS TO ENGINEERING

8 Ways
to Support Diversity, Equity, and Inclusion for All

FROM ATHLETICS TO ENGINEERING

8 Ways
to Support
Diversity, Equity,
and Inclusion
for All

❖

JOHNNIE JOHNSON & DR. MICHAEL E. WEBBER

Johnnie Johnson and Michael E. Webber

From Athletics to Engineering:

8 Ways to Support Diversity, Equity, and Inclusion for All

ISBN (Print Edition): 978-1-09835-478-7

ISBN (eBook Edition): 978-1-09835-479-4

We dedicate this book to everyone who has carried, is carrying, or will carry the baton forward in the multigenerational relay toward a more civil society.

Contents

Teresa's Foreword   1

Michael's Prologue: White Speechlessness   5

Johnnie's Prologue: The Road Is Rocky   11

Introduction   17

Chapter 1: It Starts With Each of Us   21

Chapter 2: Love Your Neighbor   35

Chapter 3: Talk About It   45

Chapter 4: Check Your Biases and Blind Spots   55

Chapter 5: Expand Your Comfort Zone   71

Chapter 6: Build Diverse Teams   81

Chapter 7: Collaborate   95

Chapter 8: Align Actions With Goals and Values   107

Epilogue   115

Acknowledgments   121

About the Authors   123

Endnotes   125

Teresa's Foreword

I am a Latina who grew up in the heart of the South with immigrant parents who were trying to assimilate to life in the U.S. and struggling to make ends meet. Similarly, Johnnie Johnson, co-author of this book, is a Black man who was raised in a small town in Texas by a single mom on welfare.

Johnnie and I have developed a special bond over our shared personal experiences and challenges that come with growing up immersed in the unconscious biases we faced then and today. Through heart-to-heart conversations where we shared anecdotes about our upbringings, race relations, racial disparities, and the role we both play in creating meaningful change, we realized how similar our lives were in many ways. Though we grew up with different genders, races, hometowns, and generations, we both had to overcome adversity and prejudices.

Despite the challenges along the way, we were able to build on the work of earlier generations to advance the cause of diversity, equity, and inclusion for all through our own examples of success. After leaving his humble beginnings, Johnnie has had thriving football, real estate, and executive coaching careers. And after leaving my humble beginnings years ago, I was appointed as the chief diversity, equity, and inclusion officer for HomeServices of America. It was Gino Blefari, the CEO of the company, who introduced me to Johnnie. HomeServices of America, a Berkshire Hathaway affiliate, is one of the largest residential real estate companies in the world, with brands such as Berkshire Hathaway HomeServices and Real Living Real Estate operating under its umbrella. The simple fact that there is a C-level executive position with a responsibility for diversity, equity, and inclusion at one of the largest real estate companies in the world is, by itself, a remarkable sign of progress. That the position is held by a Latina is also notable.

Climbing the corporate ranks in the male-dominated world of real estate has presented me with too many examples of sexism and chauvinism, which demonstrate how much further we have to go in society to reach true diversity, equity, and inclusion for all. I recognize through my personal path and professional experience that this topic is important for empowering people to reach their full potential, and I think every company and community should take the topic seriously.

So when Johnnie and his co-author Michael Webber invited me to write the foreword for this book, I was honored. I was also terrified because I'm not a writer, and this topic, while central to my life experience, is outside of my comfort zone. In fact, one of the lessons Johnnie and Michael drive home in this book is that getting outside of your comfort zone is a critical ingredient to progress because it allows us to have difficult conversations, discover self-truths, and realize that to make a difference and effect real change, we must be willing to be vulnerable. I think they're absolutely right, so I agreed.

Though I'm confident in the areas of my professional work, my personal insecurities about being good enough to write even a page in a book addressing the most daunting generational challenges in human society arose immediately. I overcame this insecurity as best I could, and I hope many of you will also not allow your insecurities to hold you back.

Reflecting on a lifetime of my personal and professional life experiences related to the broad topic of societal biases and the injustices that can result from them is a daunting but worthwhile task. These experiences took on heightened meaning when the killing of George Floyd propelled the world into a frenzy of disbelief and horror. That this killing took place in Minneapolis, where my company is headquartered, made it even more real to me. For me, this scene wasn't some abstract problem halfway around the world. Hearing the cry of this man to his own mother as he drew his last breaths was like hearing the cry of my own son, and I, too, was affected by the injustice and cruelty demonstrated that day. My passion for this subject is to make sure others do not needlessly suffer in this way.

As Michael shares in his prologue about his students and their speechlessness in the aftermath of Floyd's killing, I also witnessed speechlessness and disgruntled reactions from our white executives, owners, and real estate agents who experienced a range of emotions from anger to resentment to confusion. There was also a great deal of distrust and uncertainty. In fact, because of my position in the company as the top-ranking executive in charge of diversity and inclusion, I received numerous calls from office locations across the country requesting help with training, education, and tools to help alleviate some of the uncomfortable conversations that were taking place in our offices and homes.

Just as Michael had reached out to Johnnie to facilitate a conversation with his engineering students, I also reached out because I knew he could help me communicate with the agents as well. It was from those conversations and a sense of shared purpose among the three of us to achieve a more diverse, equitable, and inclusive world that I learned about this book.

Johnnie and Michael laid out some straightforward, logical ways to make progress that are simultaneously accessible and reasonable. Their lessons were learned from decades of coaching, mentoring, and leadership, and they can empower individuals to overcome bias, address gender, racial, or other disparities, and create a roadmap that will help guide readers along the path toward diversity, equity, and inclusion for all. Their purpose-driven framework makes me both hopeful and positive. If their ideas and strategies are widely implemented, we will make real progress toward inclusive work environments and racial harmony in all aspects of life.

I should also note that their teamwork on this—the Black athlete/ entrepreneur and the white professor/author working with mutual respect and understanding—exemplifies what they teach. The strategies they lay out take their principles and create easy paths that align actions with goals and values to ensure success and create a positive impact for those who understand this simple phrase: "Progress begins with each of us."

Teresa Palacios Smith

Minneapolis, Minnesota, USA

Michael's Prologue:
White Speechlessness

*I was scared to write this book and even discuss this
subject, but we cannot make progress if we are quiet.*

In May 2020, a smartphone video showing George Floyd's death by the hands of a white police officer captured worldwide attention. For me and my engineering students, it was a wake-up call.

I am a white professor of mechanical engineering at the University of Texas at Austin. I am also a C-level executive in Paris, France, at a global energy company, where I oversee research and innovation teams with hundreds of professionals. At the university, I supervise post-doctoral fellows, Ph.D. students, master's students, and undergraduates as they study some of society's most pressing energy and environmental problems. These students are elite. They are the best of the best.

While my group of students has included much better gender diversity than a typical engineering professor's research group, the group is historically very white. Still, we were shocked and alarmed by what we saw on that video.

At our first regularly scheduled research meeting after Floyd's death, we did not discuss research, as the students were too upset. After 15 years of advising students through events like the financial collapse of 2008, presidential elections, the COVID-19 pandemic, and the stock market meltdown in 2020, I had never seen them as distressed as they were then. While I was aware of the police brutality Black people have faced over the decades, it was in a fleeting or nonattentive way. I would pay attention when it was in the headlines but would soon forget about it as the topic faded from the news. George Floyd's death was a turning point for me. And for these students, it was their first time really seeing such an earth-shattering event.

During the group conversation, the students were scared, ashamed, guilt-ridden, angry, and eager for action. A few were teary-eyed or openly cried, which is not a typical occurrence in a weekly engineering meeting where we generally discuss research methods. It was clear the topic needed more attention. I asked if they were open to me bringing in a Black leader to facilitate a discussion with us about race in America. They readily agreed and seemed eager for the opportunity.

I reached out to Johnnie Johnson and invited him to an upcoming virtual meeting to lead us through this difficult conversation. Johnnie—the co-author of this book—is a retired NFL player who had a successful decade-long All-Pro career with the Los Angeles Rams and Seattle Seahawks. Since 2009, Johnnie has coached my students and me, joining us at some of our group meetings to lead exercises on leadership development and collaboration. He also worked one-on-one with me and several of my students for deeper development of the skills we need for success. So, in late June 2020, Johnnie joined us for a 90-minute conversation, sharing anecdotes of racism he had endured, including times he had been pulled over by white cops in his neighborhood. (It seemed like the police officers were perpetually looking for a criminal that matched his description.) He discussed the role of Black athletes in social justice—Muhammad Ali, Colin Kaepernick, and Kareem Abdul-Jabbar come to mind—and he also shared other stories of prejudice and bias.

The biggest takeaway from that conversation was my students' silence. Think about this: These students are all accomplished. They were the best students in their high schools and college classes. It's hard to find people who have more intellectual potential. These students, who always have something smart to say, all of a sudden were speechless. They were stunned and afraid to speak, both of which are rare in my observation. They went from empowered voices to timid and quiet listeners.

After the conversation, I received many unsolicited comments from my students about how great the conversation was and how helpful they found it. Clearly, Johnnie touched a nerve. But why the silence?

They were afraid of saying the wrong thing and offending our guest. They did not feel sure-footed. They were out of their comfort zone. Instead of discussing computer codes and optimization algorithms, we were dealing with human egos, emotions, biases, and behaviors, all of which are harder to model and predict. They felt an intense desire to help, to do something, but they lacked the confidence to know they would do no harm, even if they were well meaning.

From that conversation, Johnnie asked me to write a book with him that would help others address racial disparities and move toward diversity, equity, and inclusion for all. I politely demurred. After all, why should I write a book about racial harmony? This is outside of my field. Besides, there are so many experts who know so much and whose voices need to be elevated. Why would a white male engineering professor be a useful contributor to the national dialogue on race?

The answer? Because it's hard and awkward. And I'm not the only one who feels this way.

I have written multiple books and hundreds of articles in prominent papers and magazines, given speeches to audiences of thousands, and testified in front of some of the nation's most powerful people on sensitive or politicized subjects, such as climate change. I am a man of words and someone known for sharing my voice far and wide, even on sensitive or complex subjects. I am not known for shying away from controversy or nuance.

But just as my students went silent when given the opportunity to speak, I wanted to go silent. I was afraid to speak. Afraid to offend. Afraid to admit what my experience with racism might be. Perhaps, deep down, I did not want to acknowledge that as a white man and the son of a university professor, I'm more likely to be a perpetrator or a beneficiary of racial bias than its victim.

Johnnie pointed out that my and my students' silence was eerily similar and not helpful in the movement toward diversity, equity, and inclusion for all. Rather, my sudden timidity is all too common. In fact, many of you reading this might have reacted the same way if you were suddenly asked to share your thoughts about racial disparities either out loud or on paper for a public audience. On the outside, as a published author, professor, and corporate executive, I look accomplished and poised. But when it comes to these difficult conversations about race, I am unsure and anxious.

After I agreed to co-author this book with Johnnie, I felt like I had just taken on my scariest professional responsibility to date: I'm going to talk about race and prejudice. Publicly. And on purpose. It's outside my expertise and my comfort zone, but it's part of my experience—and I'm not alone on that. It is probably outside of your expertise and comfort zone too.

I hope that by making myself vulnerable and sharing my bumbling awkwardness, you will join me and Johnnie on this journey toward successful diversity and racial harmony in the workplace and society. If we recognize we all have a role to play, love our neighbors, talk about the issues, check our biases and blind spots, expand our comfort zones, build diverse teams, collaborate, and align our actions with our goals and values, we will discover we are closer than we think to making real progress.

Michael E. Webber

Austin, Texas, USA, and Paris, France

Johnnie's Prologue:
The Road Is Rocky

Michael Webber and I share a long and unexpected relationship. I have worked with him and his research group of elite engineering students on leadership and teamwork for more than a decade. Although athletics and engineering seem to be worlds apart, they have more similarities than many people realize.

After George Floyd's death by a police officer in May 2020, I received an invitation from Michael to facilitate a meeting with his students. Speaking to his group is not an unusual occurrence, but what was unique about this request was its topic: race, racism, and racial disparities. I enthusiastically accepted the invitation because I thought my personal experiences as a Black man might be of interest to his group of mostly white students.

One of the points I emphasized was the importance of developing roadmaps for our desired destination. That theme is central to my decades of coaching. It's common to use GPS (Global Positioning System) on a phone or in a car. In doing so, the user enters a desired location, and the GPS uses satellites in space to offer guidance along the way. Likewise, we need to map out figuratively where we want to go in life.

Under normal circumstances, the path to our goals is rocky. We may encounter obstacles and barriers that can potentially hinder us on our route. However, with sufficient information and a clear view of where we desire to go, a detailed roadmap can ultimately guide us to our destination. Just as road closures or detours hinder our progress by car, doubts, fears, or biases driven by our beliefs, habits, attitudes, or expectations might pose the greatest impediments for our journey toward diversity, equity, and inclusion in society. Sometimes these obstacles emerge naturally, and other times, people are actively working in opposition. Encountering challenges during the journey is not specific to any race, gender, ethnicity, or any other classification, though the severity and nature of the obstacles and privileges will vary from group to group.

If you're reading this book, perhaps you share our desire for diversity, equity, and inclusion for all in the workplace and in our communities—not just for any particular race or ethnic group but for all groups, socioeconomic classes, gender identities, ages, abilities, and orientations. Although we still have a long way to go, we are closer to our destination than some might think. I understand this might be difficult to see during turbulent times, but please stay with us.

As a nation, our GPS for everyday life is the United States Constitution as well as federal and state laws. For example, in 1964, the Civil Rights Act was passed and signed into law, prohibiting discrimination based on race, color, religion, sex, or national origin. The act outlawed segregation, banned employment discrimination in public places, and federally funded community programs. Though these and other laws were passed over the years to support diversity, equity, and inclusion for all, they were not applied uniformly. As a result, they bring race to the forefront of our national GPS.

Race is never an easy topic to discuss. It can trigger divergent emotions and biased worldviews. As a result, emotions within marginalized communities range from disappointment to frustration and anger. Marginalized communities have dealt with social, educational, and economic inequalities for decades, even centuries, and the presence of social injustice videos keeps these unfortunate hierarchical truths at the forefront of their minds, fanning the flames of these emotions even more.

When I was around a football field, basketball court, track, or baseball field as a young Black athlete, I was seen as someone who belonged. I was perceived by coaches, parents, and fans alike as an asset to the sport from an athletic standpoint. I resembled what a stereotypical elite athlete was supposed to look like. Tall, athletic, male, and Black. I was typecast, and one of my obstacles on the path toward pursuing my vision and mission was escaping this stereotype.

Those stereotypes accompanied me as I grew into adulthood. As a grown Black man, I have been pulled over by the police five times for no apparent reason—or at least no specific reason that would lead me to believe one of my white friends would be stopped in a similar situation. On each occasion, I was within one or two miles of my home or office. In the cases near my home, I was suspiciously questioned as to what I was doing in the neighborhood. I replied, "I live in the neighborhood, sir." Yet, my answers were not satisfactory, so I had to prove that I indeed lived where I said I lived. On each occasion, I was allowed to leave after answering a number of questions.

In the cases where I was stopped near my office, I was pulled over by plainclothes officers in unmarked cars. On each occasion, the reason given for my stop was that I resembled a suspect they were looking for. To me, that meant one thing: I was Black. On each occasion, I had to prove my identity and where I lived and worked. After going through that process each time, I was allowed to leave without further incident. In some cases, I would experience privilege on the heels of enduring such negative bias. For example, if the officer discovered I was a player for the Los Angeles Rams, I was treated differently. That privilege stood in stark contrast to the discrimination I endured just moments before, which was a relief but also concerning, as I recognized that other people of color may not receive the same treatment.

Being a police officer is one of the most challenging professions in society. The majority of men and women police officers throughout the country are dedicated to their craft. I know this because for years, I served as a lead volunteer for the Police Amateur Athletic Foundation's (PAAF) Annual Citywide Youth Track & Field Meet in San Jose, California, and have seen firsthand the many officers who serve our communities. The meet brings together boys and girls, ages 6 to 14, to compete for an opportunity to advance to the state meet in their age group. The police officers who support the PAAF represent many other great officers throughout the country, and I have a tremendous amount of respect for them and their profession.

Although I have that deep level of respect for the police, I understand all people, including police officers, have biases. These biases may cause a police officer to pull over people of color for no apparent reason other than their complexion. They can cause a resident to call the police alleging an unfounded crime when they see a Black person jogging in their neighborhood or going about their daily business in the community—their primary trigger for suspicion being the color of the person's skin.

Through the lens of a Black person, this experience is nothing new. For Black men in particular, the experience of watching women clutch their purses tighter or lock their car doors as we walk by is common enough. One difference today is more of the acts are captured on video and shared with others via social media, which heightens awareness and affirms what people of color have been saying for years.

As a world, we have made progress on this front, but we still have a long way to go. Though a person's GPS may be set to support diversity, equity, and inclusion for all, their behaviors may not reflect that. Their beliefs, habits, attitudes, and expectations enhanced by their personality, ego, and emotions are not always properly aligned with their desired outcome. That is certainly the feeling countless minorities experience. It leaves many Black people wondering if their lives matter in society.

Not everyone supports diversity, equity, and inclusion for all, and great inequalities remain. Because of ongoing biases and social, educational, and economic inequalities, many people feel left behind. The countless occurrences of police brutality against minorities, particularly against Black men, reinforces this point. But on a different front, this could also hold weight for some rural, working-class whites who feel left behind by globalization.

One of our aims with this book is to help society establish actual liberty and justice for all. To Blacks, this change is a clear demonstration that their lives matter. Indeed, that demonstration needs to be made for all. Looking globally, the situation in the United States is not unique. Because of the movement of people, goods, and services across borders, most nations are made up of people from many different ethnic groups, backgrounds, life experiences, and socioeconomic classes. With that makeup, challenges are certain to arise when attempting to make meaningful change, even if that change is for the good of all.

Despite the chaos we see throughout the nation today, we are closer than you may think to achieving our goal. One of the areas where that is most visible is in the sports world, which we will discuss further in this book.

Johnnie Johnson

San Jose, California, USA

Introduction

Athletics [ath-**le**-tiks]

Seeking to achieve a goal by applying physical skills
or capabilities, such as strength, agility, or stamina,
according to the principles of athletic training.

Engineering [en-j*uh*-**neer**-ing]

The art or science of solving problems by the practical application of
principles from disciplines, such as chemistry, biology, or physics.

Athletics and engineering might appear worlds apart, but look-ing more closely, it seems they are more similar than we think. Athletes and engineers are both rooted in solving problems and apply-ing a set of guiding principles to achieve goals. For the football team, the guiding principles are the rules of the game and the fundamentals are blocking, tackling, and protecting the football. For engineers, the relevant guidelines are determined by natural laws, such as physics or thermodynamics.

They are also inherently built around teamwork. Even athletes who compete in individual sports, such as tennis or golf, are sur-rounded by a team of trainers, coaches, nutritionists, and advisors. And the concept of the lone engineer solving problems by herself in a garage stands in rare contrast to the large teams of engineers needed to create the successful space program or operate our energy system.

Succeeding in athletics requires physical and mental strength, concentration, focus, speed, skills, and a clear understanding of physical concepts such as momentum, which is mass (body weight) multiplied by velocity (speed). This relationship makes it possible for a 200-pound defensive back, someone approximately Johnnie's size, to tackle a ball carrier with the same force as a slower-moving 300-pound lineman. Succeeding in engineering requires much of the same skillset.

In addition to momentum, a deep understanding of angles and geometry is important for athletes and engineers. As a defensive back, one of Johnnie's strengths was his understanding of which angle he needed to use to tackle a ball carrier or intercept a pass. Coaches would famously repeat the importance of taking the correct angle to stop players from opposing teams. If a defensive player misgauges the strength of a passer's arm or the runner's speed, he risks missing the tackle and having the opponent gain a lot of ground against the defense or, worse, score a touchdown.

That means football players are doing geometry on the fly while they are running so they can get their angles correct. But it's not just football. Athletes in just about every sport—baseball, basketball, hockey, tennis, golf, billiards, bowling, you name it—need to handle concepts related to momentum and angles to be successful.

Engineers also master these concepts, but do so with pencil and paper for their homework assignments or exams. By contrast, athletes—often the ones who are stereotyped as "dumb jocks"—do it in their heads while they are moving. Through this lens, it might give engineers pause to reflect on the relative difficulty of performing physics and geometry calculations in such a stressful environment and without the luxury of an eraser.

This means athletes and engineers are more similar than we might think. And this is true for every group. Humans are more similar than we think, even if we seem very different.

Despite these underlying commonalities, there are many unnecessary divisions imposed and propagated by society. These divisions hinder our ability to reach our full potential and impact all of us. Given the tensions and community dialogues surrounding disparities and inequities based on race, gender, ethnicity, religion, sexual orientation, age, and ability, the time is ripe to improve the situation.

With this book, we seek to share lessons from our decades of experience in coaching, mentoring, and leadership to lay out eight ways you can support diversity, equity, and inclusion for all at your workplace and in your community:

1. It Starts With Each of Us

2. Love Your Neighbor

3. Talk About It

4. Check Your Biases and Blind Spots

5. Expand Your Comfort Zone

6. Build Diverse Teams

7. Collaborate

8. Align Actions With Goals and Values

Some readers and their organizations are already implementing a subset of these actions. Few implement all of them, and even for those that do, there is always room for improvement.

We are not experts who conduct research on diversity, equity, and inclusion; however, we do have a lot of life experience in coaching, mentoring, leading, and building diverse teams. And we think these recommendations based on lessons we learned the hard way will make a positive impact if implemented correctly.

Ultimately, regardless of who we are, where we come from, our ethnicity, or where we fall on the socioeconomic scale, we all need protection, encouragement, inspiration, and empowerment in our lives. This is especially true with all the challenges we face when attempting to effect meaningful change in society for the good of all people. That concept is central to our decades of mentoring and coaching.

We have learned through extensive travel around the world and work with different sectors of society that at their most fundamental, people from all walks of life want the same things: security, peace, and a chance for prosperity. At our core, we are all very similar and many of the divisions by race, ethnicity, or other factors are unnecessary and distract us from our commonality.

The goal with this book is to share multiple perspectives centered on the goal of empowering people to improve their own lives and those around them. Though this book combines the personal experiences and lessons learned from an athlete and an engineer, the recommended steps should be relevant to any career and for everyday living. We recommend that readers contemplate how the anecdotes and explanations connect with their own life experiences. Importantly, this book is intended to help start the process. However, it should not be the end of the journey toward diversity, equity, and inclusion for all.

CHAPTER 1

It Starts With Each of Us

The most important first step in supporting diversity, equity, and inclusion for all is deciding to act. Committing to making progress is a precondition for success, and for systemic problems, we cannot sit around and wait for someone else to solve them. It starts with us, and we each have a role to play. The decision to take action is often the hardest step, but it's the most critical because without a commitment to improvement, the system will not get better.

Dr. Martin Luther King Jr. famously said, "The arc of the moral universe is long, but it bends toward justice." A famous quip in retort is that "the moral arc doesn't bend all by itself." In other words, we have to take action to move toward our goals. As with everything else in life that is important, waiting for someone else to solve our problems or waiting for the moral arc to bend on its own does not get us where we want to be. We have to bend it, but we do not need to bend it by ourselves, as that task is too great. In fact, we will need all of us working together to bend the universe's arc toward justice, which is why we discuss teams and collaboration later in this book. Standing aside while others do the heavy lifting or, worse, actively working against them, is not what the world is calling for. Each of us has a responsibility to decide how, when, and whether to engage. We encourage you to take that step, strengthen the team, and move us toward the destination together.

Think about what is within each of our individual spheres of influence and what we can achieve. The first step is recognizing that we each have to take action because society cannot improve itself on its own. This is where we take a page from athletics. The most productive sports teams are built with a culture of "We," "Us," and "Team," not "They," "Me," or "I"—with a notable exception: accepting responsibility for an individual's part in achieving the team success. This approach often leads to enhanced trust and a stronger bond among teammates with consistent team success.

Getting Started

For this or any other long-term process, the most difficult task for most people is simply getting started. And maybe for this topic it is even harder than normal because some people are not sure the desired outcome (a more diverse, equitable, and inclusive workplace or community) is a priority. Humans have a lot of inertia, so going from inaction to action can require significant effort. For many, the enormous size of the challenge is intimidating and gives a sense of impossibility. This feeling is one Johnnie typically saw at the start of the NFL season with his teammates' goal of winning a division championship or Super Bowl. Michael has seen this with his students starting a multiyear dissertation project for their Ph.D. Perhaps you have been daunted by your own goals, such as losing weight, taking your business to the next level, or launching your own company. There are rarely overnight successes; most of the time, it takes months or sometimes years to reach our destination. From that distance, it can be hard to get motivated and take the first step.

In addition, many people are afraid their pathway will not be perfect. The rocky path Johnnie described in his prologue will undoubtedly make its presence known. The desire for perfection combined with the enormity of the task and the duration of the process is likely to inspire procrastination despite the urgency that might be felt. The key to overcoming procrastination is to focus on taking the first step instead of fixating on the entire journey, the barriers in the way, or the difficulty of the requirements. Rather than focusing solely on the end goals, like winning a national championship, writing a 200-page dissertation, or taking your business to the next level, it's important to identify the main goal and then break down the process into many smaller steps so you can work through them one by one. Think about the next step, which is close at hand, rather than the last step, which is far away.

To win a national championship at the collegiate level, the coach knows the process begins with the first day of offseason training. They know competing schools aim for the same goal. They also know every team is operating under the same rules and guidelines that pertain to training, practice, and game schedules. To put their team in the best position to win the national championship, every coach begins the process by taking the first step. They set a mini goal they desire to accomplish on the first day of training, then turn their full focus to achieving that goal. Whether or not they accomplish their goal for that day, they evaluate their process, adjust as necessary, and turn their full attention to their goal for the next day. They continue this process throughout the season until, at such time, two teams compete for the right to be crowned the champion.

Breaking down big goals into a series of smaller, manageable objectives makes it less intimidating to get started. This is key for our goal of diversity, equity, and inclusion for all, but it applies to most other goals in life too.

Start Where You Are

Another key aspect of this is to start where you are. A lot of people are daunted because their destination seems so far away, but no one starts at the destination. Start where you are, then make steady progress toward the goal.

Johnnie learned a great deal from his many years in the NFL, competing against some of the greatest athletes in the world. As such, he understands that the process to goal attainment is slow and steady, and it starts with where you are today. The life lessons he learned from being coached and competing against the teams of some of legendary coaches squarely imprinted his understanding that goal attainment is a process of many daily incremental action steps, not simply a destination. This process applies to all aspects of our lives. No coach would put their team through one offseason training session or one regular season practice and expect them to be ready to compete for a championship. No sales manager would establish a sales quota with a new sales associate and expect them to hit it in one day.

When you plug a destination into your GPS, it gives you an estimated time of arrival at your desired destination that is based on your starting point in relation. Starting where you are is a vitally important part of the goal attainment process because it helps determine what fundamental activities are necessary to achieve your aims. In all aspects of our lives, it is the consistency with which we practice those activities with faith and perseverance that provides us the opportunity to achieve our goals. This is also the case as we pursue diversity, equity, and inclusion for all.

It Doesn't End With Each of Us

Though supporting diversity, equity, and inclusion starts with each of us, it does not end with each of us. We are not, and should not be, alone in this endeavor. Rather, our work is part of a team spanning many countries and centuries. Progress is slow, and we need to keep it moving forward.

The Olympics provides some teachable examples. Because the Olympics draws teams from around the world and because the different skills required to compete vary so much from sport to sport, it is a prominent celebration of remarkable racial, ethnic, religious, and physical diversity. The athletes come in all different sizes and ages, and from various socioeconomic backgrounds. When petite gymnasts stand next to tall basketball players or stout discus throwers walk alongside lanky runners during opening ceremonies, it is clear these elite athletes belong despite their obvious physical differences. But it wasn't always that way.

Jesse Owens, a Black man on Team USA, achieved international fame at the 1936 Summer Olympics in Berlin, Germany, by winning gold medals in four track and field events: 100 meters, 200 meters, long jump, and 4x100-meter relay. When he and his teammates won the 4x100-meter relay, they did so in a then world record time of 39.8 seconds. This remarkable feat was accomplished under adverse circumstances. At the time, in his deeply segregated home country, he was unable to sleep, dine with, or accompany his white Olympic teammates. In Germany, he was allowed to stay in the same hotels, but was still subjected to racist taunts by the Nazi regime that hosted the competition. Jesse Owens' fourth gold medal in the relay race is a fitting parable for the challenge of supporting diversity, equity, and inclusion.

In the relay race, four teammates are required to collectively run 400 meters. Each team member runs 100 meters before passing a handheld baton to another teammate. The lead runner passes to the second leg, who passes to the third leg, and finally, the baton is passed to the anchor leg or the fourth runner, who completes the competition by covering the last 100 meters of the race. Speed is of paramount importance but so is the passing of the baton. If the baton is dropped, the team loses. As such, the winning team has both the fastest runners and smoothest handoffs.

As one of the top athletes in the United States during his high school career, Johnnie was recruited by or received scholarship offers from more than 100 different colleges and universities around the United States in four different sports. He chose to accept a scholarship to play football at the University of Texas at Austin. Like the public school system in his hometown of La Grange, Texas, the university's student body was predominately white. The UT varsity football team did not allow its first Black player until 1970. By the time Johnnie joined the team in 1976, it included several Black star athletes, including Heisman Trophy winner Earl Campbell. Another Black teammate, Johnny "Lam" Jones, arrived that fall, fresh off of winning a gold medal for the United States as an 18-year-old on the 4x100-meter relay team at the 1976 Olympics in Montreal, Canada.

After a successful career at Texas as a two-time consensus All-American in football, Johnnie went on to become the number one draft pick for the Los Angeles Rams in the 1980 NFL Draft. Both Jones (New York Jets) and Derrick Hatchett (Baltimore Colts) joined him as first-round picks in the 1980 draft to give the University of Texas three Black first-round draft picks in the same draft, just 10 years after the first Black player joined the team. The pace of progress after athletics integrated was more rapid than many other sectors of society.

With the Los Angeles Rams, Johnnie played with another Olympic gold medal winner: Ron Brown, who was a member of the United States 4x100-meter relay team in the 1984 Summer Games in Los Angeles, California. Like Jesse Owens' race before, that 4x100-meter relay team also broke the world record. With that victory, fellow relay runner Carl Lewis earned his fourth gold medal of the 1984 Summer Olympic Games, matching Jesse Owens from the 1936 Games decades before. Interestingly, both Jones and Brown were wide receivers, so as a defensive back, Johnnie spent much of his practices during his college and NFL careers keeping up with two of the world's fastest runners. Having watched his now-teammates earn Olympic glory, Johnnie had a front row seat to what it took to run a successful relay. Critically, for the relay team, it is the handoff of the baton from one runner to the next that has the biggest potential to differentiate between a gold medal and disqualification. A successful handoff keeps the team moving forward at full speed. A dropped baton causes forward progress to stop.

We each have to do our part, we each have a role on the team, and we each have to pass the baton from one generation to the next. For the United States, it can be said that the relay race for liberty and justice for all began in 1775 with the start of the Revolutionary War, then followed by the writing of the Declaration of Independence, Constitution, and Bill of Rights. While these were all important steps in the right direction, they left out women, enslaved people, and Indigenous people. Even the label often used in history books to describe the group of people we celebrate from this era—the Founding Fathers—is exclusive to white men and obscures the contributions of Abigail Adams, Dolley Madison, Mercy Otis Warren, Eliza Hamilton, and other important Revolutionary-War era white women.

Though the Bill of Rights enshrined many civil liberties into law, the push for diversity, equity, and inclusion was not complete, so the effort to move it forward was handed off to the next generation. Thankfully, the U.S. Constitution gives a framework for the continual process of baton-passing through the addition of various amendments and the creation of other laws.

Many critical issues, such as slavery and women's rights, were not addressed fairly in the Revolutionary Era; rather they were punted to future generations. After Abraham Lincoln was elected president of the United States in 1860, 11 Southern states that supported slavery left the Union and became the Confederate States of America. This disagreement over slavery led to the Civil War between the Northern and Southern states, which lasted from 1861 to 1865. During this era, Lincoln issued the Emancipation Proclamation, which laid the groundwork for the eventual freedom of slaves across the country. Ultimately, the Northern states defeated the Southern states, those that left the Union were readmitted to the United States, and the Thirteenth, Fourteenth, and Fifteenth Amendments to the Constitution— known as the Civil War Amendments—were added. The Thirteenth Amendment abolished slavery in the United States except as punish- ment for a crime; the Fourteenth Amendment guaranteed that citizens would receive equal protection under the law and granted citizenship to anyone born in the United States, including former slaves; and the Fifteenth Amendment granted Black men the right to vote. Though still incomplete in many ways—notably, women's right to vote was not included in these amendments—the successful passing of the baton from the Revolutionary War-era to the Civil War generation was critical forward progress in the direction of liberty and justice for all.

To be clear, the baton can be and has been dropped. Though the Civil War Amendments granted basic civil rights, struggles to secure federal protection of those rights continued. The Jim Crow laws in the late 19th through mid-20th centuries were a significant slowdown and even a step backward because of the way they facilitated unequal treatment toward nonwhites in the South. Jim Crow laws were state and local statutes that legalized racial segregation. The laws marginalized Blacks by denying them the right to get an education, vote, hold certain jobs, or take advantage of other opportunities through various discriminatory practices based solely on their race. The laws existed for decades until a series of new laws was passed in the 1960s. In the meantime, the ugly actions exhibited by some people and institutions at the time did not align with the stated values of the Civil War Amendments. After the Civil War, the baton was passed multiple times to different people and causes, ultimately producing the Nineteenth Amendment, the civil rights movement, and the passing of civil rights legislation in 1866, 1871, 1875, 1957, 1960, 1964, 1965 and 1968.

After a long-standing effort by the women's suffrage movement, the Nineteenth Amendment passed in 1920, prohibiting the states and federal government from denying the right to vote to citizens of the United States on account of sex. While many newspapers in 2020 celebrated the 100th anniversary of suffrage and women's right to vote, the articles and headlines rarely clarified that, practically speaking, the Nineteenth Amendment only guaranteed the right of *white* women to vote. Nonwhite women did not have their right to vote protected until the Voting Rights Act of 1965. The generations that received the handoff during the civil rights era from 1866 to the 1960s continued to face many challenges when attempting to get various civil rights laws passed during that time, but they continued to run with determination. Collectively, the legislation led to the banning of racial discrimination and greater social and economic mobility while ensuring greater access to resources for women, minorities, and low-income families.

The civil rights movement in the mid-20th century was led by heroic Black activists, like Dr. King and Rosa Parks. In December 1955 in Montgomery, Alabama, Rosa Parks refused to give up her seat in the back of the bus (where Black people were supposed to sit) to a white man after the white-only section was filled. She was arrested for civil disobedience, as she had violated Alabama's segregationist laws. Her willingness to confront bus segregation inspired the city's Black community to boycott the Montgomery buses. Dr. King led the boycott, and as Blacks made up a substantial portion of the ridership, the boycott made an impact on the bus system's revenues. Parks' case went to court, and in a separate 1956 decision, it was ruled that bus segregation is unconstitutional under the Equal Protection Clause of the Fourteenth Amendment. With that ruling, our nation was one step closer to liberty and justice for all in reality.

Eloquent, smart, and inspirational, Dr. King was a minister and activist who became the most visible Black spokesperson and leader of the civil rights movement as it rose in national prominence during the mid-1950s. Among a lifetime of notable moments, Dr. King helped organize the 1963 March on Washington, where he delivered his famous "I Have a Dream" speech on the steps of the Lincoln Memorial. Rosa Parks and Dr. King were both critical members of the multigenerational relay to diversity, equity, and inclusion. And this is an important point: It's not only the famous, once-in-a-century leaders like Dr. King who play a role, it's also the everyday citizens like Rosa Parks who are critical to passing the baton forward.

Through the participation of millions of individuals, Congress got the message and passed the Civil Rights Act of 1964, prohibiting discrimination on the basis of race, color, religion, sex (at least in Title VII), or national origin. The act prohibited discrimination in interstate commerce and federally funded programs. It also strengthened the enforcement of voting rights and the desegregation of schools. The passage of the act outlawed Jim Crow laws that propagated racial segregation. In 1965, the Voting Rights Act, which prohibited racial discrimination in voting, was signed into law by President Lyndon B. Johnson. Further progress was made with the Fair Housing Act of 1968, which prohibited discrimination concerning the sale, rental, and financing of housing based on race, religion, or national origin. The act was expanded in 1974 to include sex/gender. These political developments were important in establishing legal frameworks. But there was also visible progress occurring in the sports world, as Blacks began breaking the color barrier in various professional leagues. We already introduced Jesse Owens' Olympic heroics from 1936, but there were heroes in other professional sports as well.

Jackie Robinson was the first Black to play baseball in the major leagues, joining the Brooklyn Dodgers in 1947, though Moses Fleetwood Walker and his brother Weldy Walker predated Robinson, playing for Toledo in the American Association in 1884. After a ban on Blacks, Kenny Washington became one of two players to reintegrate the NFL when he signed with the Los Angeles Rams in 1946, the football team Johnnie would join 34 years later. Chuck Cooper (Boston Celtics), Nat Clifton (New York Knicks), and Earl Lloyd (Washington Capitals) were among the first Blacks to play in the NBA in 1950, though Harry Lew, who was also Black, played for the less-prominent New England Professional Basketball League in 1902. Althea Gibson became the first Black woman tennis player to compete in a U.S. national competition in 1950. Willie O'Ree became the first Black player in the National Hockey League in 1958. Bill Russell became the first Black coach in the NBA when he was named player-coach of the Boston Celtics in 1966. Tiger Woods became the first nonwhite winner of the Master's Tournament in 1997. That tournament is hosted by the

Augusta National Golf Club, which admitted its first Black member just a few years before in 1990.

Was Jackie Robinson really the first Black player good enough to play with whites? Or rather, was he simply the first Black player the white power structure allowed into the league? Without a doubt, Jackie Robinson was a special player, but the white managers and owners also had a role in receiving the baton and passing it on. Indeed, it's critical for members of the dominant culture to be helpful allies for this progression. As Robin DiAngelo explains in her book *White Fragility*, women seeking suffrage could not grant it to themselves.[1] They could not vote in favor of suffrage because they did not have the right to vote. White men with the right to vote had to participate in their inclusion. That means members of the white male power structure have to be a part of the relay race.

When Barack Obama was elected president in 2008, many people concluded that our challenges with race relations were solved. They had to be. After all, we just elected the first Black president in the history of the United States. In fact, it is not uncommon for people to point to the Emancipation Proclamation of 1863, the Civil Rights Act of 1964, or President Obama's election in 2008 as evidence that discrimination and racial biases no longer exist. Certainly, that election was a historic moment. But President Obama is just one man, and the prevailing white male representation in other power structures, such as the Supreme Court, U.S. Senate, and governors' mansions, undermines claims that the nation has become post-racial or that the gender divide has been fully bridged.

Although he held a very powerful position, he could not run the relay by himself. President Obama needed committed allies alongside him to build off the progress of earlier leaders before handing the baton to the next generation. After President Obama's second term, Hillary Clinton, who served as U.S. Secretary of State from 2009 to 2013, became the first woman to be nominated for president of the United States by a major political party when she won the Democratic Party nomination in 2016. She would go on to win the popular vote but lose the electoral vote to President Donald Trump.

In 2020, when Joe Biden, who served as President Obama's vice president, secured the Democratic Party's presidential nomination, he made history by selecting Kamala Harris as his running mate. She was not the first major-party female vice-presidential nominee, as the Republican and Democratic parties both had female VP candidates in prior elections: former Alaska Governor Sarah Palin in 2008 and former U.S. Representative Geraldine Ferraro in 1984. But Harris is the first elected. And the first Black woman and first person of Indian descent to be nominated for national office by a major political party in the United States, much less to win. (Harris' father is from Jamaica and her mother is from India.)

Think about that for a moment. In a span of 12 years, from 2008 to 2020, we saw the first Black man serve as president of the United States, the first woman to be nominated for president of the United States by a major political party, and the first Black woman and first person of Indian descent to be nominated for and elected to national office by a major party in the United States. Just a few decades earlier, some of these major party candidates did not have the right to vote.

Unfortunately, pushback against national inclusion reveals itself in many ways. The rise in hate crimes against Asian-Americans in the wake of the COVID-19 pandemic, emboldened white supremacists, and elimination of training programs on diversity in the federal government and corporations with federal contracts all make clear that much work remains. But if we recognize that we all have a role to play and we work together, we can make continuous improvement and progress toward our collective goals. When the baton is passed to us, we need to be ready to run with it.

CHAPTER 2

Love Your Neighbor

If you distill the world's major faiths down to their core essentials, they all basically have two fundamental concepts: 1) believe in something bigger than yourself and 2) love one another. These are useful words to live by, and they are expressed in different forms. In Christianity, the idea that we should "love our neighbors as ourselves" is one of the Ten Commandments. The more common manifestation globally is the Golden Rule, which says we should treat everyone the way we wish to be treated.

According to Rushworth Kidder, an esteemed author and founder of the Institute for Global Ethics, the core idea of the Golden Rule prominently appears in every major religion, including Buddhism, Islam, Judaism, Christianity, Hinduism, Taoism, and Zoroastrianism.[2] Philosophy professor Simon Blackburn also notes that the Golden Rule has roots in early Confucianism (around 500 BCE) and can be "found in some form in almost every ethical tradition."[3]

If the Golden Rule's tenet to love others as we wish for them to love us is good enough for every religion and ethical tradition, then it is a great place to start in moving closer to diversity, equity, and inclusion for all. Note that commandments such as "Love your neighbor" do not say to "love your neighbors, but only if they have the same skin color." But, as is often said, "love your neighbor" was always the hardest of the commandments to follow. There will surely be plenty of obstacles in your way.

Know Your Neighbor

Before you can love your neighbors, you have to recognize who your neighbors are. That is, you have to know your community. If we fall victim to our biases and blind spots, we might fail to recognize that someone is a part of our community. This can cause harm in a variety of ways.

In the early 1980s, when now-prominent astrophysicist Neil deGrasse Tyson was a student at the University of Texas at Austin, university police stopped and questioned him on his way to the physics building seven times. He was never stopped or questioned on the way to the gym.[4] The physics building and gym are in different parts—that is, different neighborhoods—of campus. This anecdote shows that the police considered it suspicious for a Black man to enter the physics building but perfectly normal for him to go to the gym. Racially biased stereotypes that Black people are athletes and white people are researchers can influence decision-making about who belongs in which neighborhood on campus.

In June 2020, James Juanillo, a Filipino-American who lives in a posh neighborhood in San Francisco, posted signs and messages at his residence in support of the Black Lives Matter movement. A white couple intervened and told him vandalism was a crime, thinking he did not live in the house. When he asked how the couple knew he didn't reside in the property, they said they knew the resident, which was clearly wrong as Juanillo had lived in the property for 18 years. The couple called the police, but the officers did not get out of their car after arriving, as they recognized Juanillo. In this example, the white couple did not even know who their neighbors were, yet the cops knew. To be brief, it's hard to love your neighbor if you don't even *know* your neighbors.

Fred Rogers was the beloved host of *Mr. Rogers' Neighborhood*, the popular children's show that aired on PBS for more than three decades. The primary theme of the show was to be a good neighbor, and his signature line was, "Won't you be my neighbor?" Essentially, his message was that we should all be each other's neighbor, which involves looking out for one another, as we are all part of the same community. Ultimately, everyone on the planet is your neighbor. To truly make substantial progress in achieving diversity, equity, and inclusion for all—or any other priority—we must take the time to know our neighbors, then love them.

Don't Divide and Isolate Your Neighborhoods

Over many decades in various cities, discriminatory urban design, transportation planning, housing policies, and lending practices created isolated or divided neighborhoods. It was not unusual for property deeds in certain neighborhoods to include restrictive covenants that prevented homeowners from selling their houses to Jews or nonwhites.[5] During the buildout of the national interstate highway system in the 1950s, urban stretches of the multilane highways created a new barrier that made it harder for people to cross by foot or bicycle from one neighborhood to another. In cities like Austin, Texas, and elsewhere, the highways were built in such a way that exacerbated the divide between the Black and white parts of town. In prior decades, railways created similar divisions and gave rise to the popular terminology in labeling someone's upbringing as undesirable by claiming they came from "the wrong side of the tracks."

Bank lenders exacerbated the isolation of neighborhoods by using a practice called redlining to identify in which neighborhoods it would be easier or harder to get home improvement loans or mortgages to purchase a property. White neighborhoods were ranked more favorably than minority neighborhoods, which created a self-propagating cycle. Homeowners could gain access to money to improve their homes in white neighborhoods, whereas nonwhite homeowners in minority neighborhoods were left out, creating a situation where the better neighborhoods improved steadily and run-down neighborhoods spiraled downward. These systemic differences aggravated the divide. Combined with the racially restrictive covenants, it became increasingly difficult for Black homeowners to move out of their run-down neighborhoods into the better neighborhoods. Overlaid with these rules were gender biases that made it difficult for women to open bank accounts or get loans without a man—usually a husband or father—included in the process.

The rise of the suburbs after World War II and the "white flight" phenomenon of white families moving out of cities into these new neighborhoods intensified divides yet again. In this case, white families had the mobility to move from one neighborhood to another, with the additional access to capital to improve their new neighborhood. Yet, nonwhite families did not have that freedom of movement nor access to capital, becoming instead trapped in urban neighborhoods destined for decline by the combination of unfair housing, transportation, and lending practices.

In modern American parlance, this concept of densely populated, inner-city, poor, minority neighborhoods is captured by the term "ghetto." A ghetto doesn't sound like the type of neighborhood most people would want to live in because of its negative connotations. The word likely has its roots in the 1500s from the Jewish neighborhood in Venice, Italy. During the Holocaust, Germany's Nazi regime created more than 1,000 ghettos to contain Jewish and Roma populations before they were shipped to concentration camps. This dark history shows that intentionally dividing groups and isolating them into neighborhoods can lead to bad outcomes. But rather than dividing and isolating our neighborhoods, what if we ensured everyone could move freely from one neighborhood to another? What if everyone felt welcome in every neighborhood? What if everyone had the same access to capital to improve their neighborhoods? Various fair housing and lending legislation in the 1960s tackled some of these issues, but the physical barriers, such as highways, and the cultural barriers, such as prevailing home values, continue to propagate some of the discrepancies.

For the engineering disciplines, one of these lasting discrepancies was gender division. After World War II, most major American universities expanded enrollment and increased their research efforts. In fact, the concept of the modern research university did not exist before the war. The post-war research boom was mostly in engineering and the sciences; it lasted decades. There was a major expansion of buildings and facilities on campuses to accommodate the influx of students and the specialized equipment needed for experimental research. In addition to classrooms, universities added laboratories, machine shops, glassblowing facilities, and other support systems for the researchers.

Michael took the majority of his classes as an undergraduate aerospace engineering student in a building constructed in 1959. It was state-of-the-art when it was built in the wake of the Sputnik launch in 1957, which kicked off the Space Race between the United States and the Soviet Union. This building had every advanced research capability that could have been desired at the time, but it did not have bathrooms for women. It's as if it simply did not occur to anyone—the dean of the engineering college, the department chairman, the architect, or the construction company—that women would ever set foot in the building. By the time Michael was a student decades later, this problem was rectified by converting the bathrooms on alternative floors into men's and women's restrooms, creating an awkward situation where students would need to ascend or descend a level to get to the restroom, depending on the floor they were already on. Engineering departments in the 1970s and later recognized that women also excel at engineering, so buildings from that era were built with men's and women's rooms on each floor. That building served as a neighborhood for aerospace engineering students, faculty, and researchers, but the way it was designed sent a signal that particular groups—in this case, women—were not welcome.

Interestingly, bathrooms are often used to determine who belongs where. Throughout the segregationist Southern states, whites and nonwhites had separate bathrooms, along with water fountains, restaurants, and other public spaces. The book *Hidden Figures* by Margot Lee Shetterly[6] captures some of these challenges. The book features the story of several Black women who were excellent mathematicians. Despite many race and gender obstacles in their way, their math skills were too good to ignore, so NASA managers included them on all-male, all-white teams as part of the collective effort to win the Space Race against the Soviets. However, because they were in the segregated South, they could not use the bathrooms in the same building as their colleagues, creating memorable scenes in the movie adaptation, in which the lead character Katherine Johnson—who later received the Presidential Medal of Freedom at the White House in 2015 and is the namesake of the Katherine G. Johnson Computational Research Facility at NASA's Langley Research Center in Virginia—runs across the sprawling NASA campus in heels, despite the weather, to a building that had bathrooms for nonwhites. Though she was invited into the neighborhood of the white male engineers for the sake of her work, the segregated bathrooms and lunchrooms propagated societal divisions and were a reminder that the invitation was limited. Even after several civil rights laws were introduced to eradicate this kind of socialization, there continues to be a national dialogue regarding the use of public toilets by transgendered individuals.

Whether it's bathrooms or highways, we use our structures and systems both unintentionally and intentionally to send a signal about who belongs in our neighborhood. Opening up our neighborhood and expanding our view of who our neighbors are will enable all of us to contribute to improving the neighborhood and strengthening our communities and teams. NASA opening up their computational team to include Black women improved their ability to perform the calculations they needed for human spaceflight.

Shared Spaces and Shared Successes Can Be a Pathway Toward Inclusion

Johnnie's first lessons with the concept of loving your neighbor began with his mother's teachings at home. As a child, he was encouraged to participate in extracurricular activities at school and on the playground in the neighborhood where he grew up. Johnnie was born in the segregated South and was raised by a single parent, the late Jessie Mae Johnson, in a poor family of 11 children in La Grange, a small rural town in central Texas. La Grange only had a few thousand residents at the time, and one of his early memories of its downtown was a store that had a sign in the front window that read: "No Coloreds Allowed." When Johnnie asked what the sign said, his mother simply said they weren't welcome there.

Though the Civil Rights Act outlawed such discrimination a short time later, the feeling of exclusion lingers to this day. We all have experiences of being left out of a conversation, not being invited to a party, or getting selected last for the kickball team at school recess. For many minorities, that feeling of exclusion is felt with a frequent rhythm throughout the course of everyday life. Our job today is to work toward inclusion, eliminating exclusion, and avoiding making people feel unwanted.

Despite the challenges of raising a large family on her own in this setting, Johnnie's mother instilled deep-rooted values, character, and life skills in her children as they grew up. A woman of strong faith, her mission in life was to raise her children to be the best they could be, despite the challenges that would emerge. She was the single greatest influence in his life, with many schoolteachers, sports coaches, and school counselors helping along the way.

When Johnnie started elementary school, the La Grange public school system was still segregated, so he began in an all-Black school. He and the other Black kids were all taught in a two-room schoolhouse for students in grades one through six, which was hardly an environment where a teacher was positioned to provide a quality education.

Despite many prevailing negative stereotypes that people of color people are lazy, do not want to work, only want handouts such as welfare, or don't want to improve themselves, the truth is quite the opposite. The key is access and opportunity. Providing a platform for a quality education was something many minority parents had been seeking for years so their children could elevate their positions in society and secure better jobs. They weren't looking to avoid work; they were looking for better opportunities for their children to have *more* schoolwork at a higher standard.

When those rights were protected as part of the 1964 Civil Rights Act, integration of public schools followed. When the integration first took place for Johnnie just before the second grade, his educational neighborhood expanded. Johnnie entered his all-white school with trepidation and fear for himself and his younger siblings, who would take their turn after him in the years to follow. Even after he and other Black classmates enrolled, the school remained predominantly white. This new school was different. In the white school, there was a dedicated classroom for each grade level and a specialized teacher and textbook for each subject. This was all new, as Johnnie did not have those benefits at the all-Black school. This more diverse academic neighborhood provided him with access to better educational resources.

Another inclusive neighborhood was the playground during school recess. On the playground and the school's athletic fields, students of all colors mingled more readily and naturally. It was also during this integrated playtime that Johnnie started to discover his athletic talents. A similar phenomenon happened at the city's parks and playgrounds. The children, left to their own devices, would happily play with each other. The exclusions and discrimination would only crop up when parents were present, suggesting that prejudices are taught rather than inherently known.

It is notable that the sports fields at the school and in the city were where integration happened most readily. That suggests sports—or more generally, play and other social activities—are a natural way to build trust and friendships. That is why parks and other shared public spaces are a central element of urban design. Designing our neighborhoods and schools for such inclusive spaces is important for advancing toward the goals of this book. Designing our communities and spaces to exclude, or allowing legacy barriers to remain, greatly inhibit our progress.

Junior high school is when Johnnie began competing in sports because they were offered through the school free of charge, enabling participation by everyone, including poor Black kids. Through this combined experience of integrating into an all-white school and joining sports teams, Johnnie developed new friendships across an academically and ethnically diverse group. They committed to sticking together as student athletes throughout their entire high school career, with some even remaining friends to this day. Despite whatever barriers were present in their small town, the playing fields and the locker room made up an inclusive neighborhood, and the result spilled out into the surrounding city.

After years of steady improvement, during his senior year, Johnnie's football team made it to the state championship game in Abilene, Texas, a five-hour drive away. The team's success brought the city together in a way that made it seem like racial barriers had never existed. The entire town shut down on game day so everyone could attend, whites and Blacks alike. Buses were chartered for the drive so even poor residents could cheer on the team as the La Grange High School won its first state championship in football. This anecdote shows how inclusion on the field can also lead to inclusion in society as a whole if the other stakeholders—in this case, the fans—feel a common purpose with the participants and a shared sense of their success. We must expand our view of our various neighborhoods and work to make them inclusive, giving a chance for broader participation and success to develop.

If we get to know and love our neighbors, avoiding the creation of false divisions and barriers that inhibit the flow in society, we can strengthen our communities and make progress toward diversity, equity, and inclusion for all.

CHAPTER 3

Talk About It

If we are going to talk about racial, ethnic, or gender disparities in society, who gets to talk about them? In brief, everyone. We cannot leave the conversation to just experts, people of color, or other members of marginalized communities. Why not? Because most people are not experts, and many people are not marginalized. Also, we can't leave it to the experts or marginalized groups as they aren't necessarily in the room nor do they have the power and privilege to break down the discriminatory and biased systems. In particular, we need members of the entrenched power structure—the very ones who need to be more inclusive—to be a part of the process. If we artificially narrow who gets to participate in the conversation, it will be harder to make substantial progress, as the lessons must be learned broadly to promote positive momentum. Movement toward diversity, equity, and inclusion will be more long-lasting if it happens in unison rather than in a haphazard or disjointed way.

When Johnnie and Michael decided to write this book, one of the first steps they both took was soliciting reactions and feedback from family, friends, mentors, trusted advisors, and community leaders. While both of them received support and encouragement, there was a difference in the reactions they received. Johnnie received enthusiastic support from mostly everyone he spoke with. In particular, they encouraged him to add his voice to the national conversation because the insights of a former professional athlete and successful Black entrepreneur were sorely missing. Michael also received encouragement, but with a very different tone and with words of hesitation or caution often mixed in.

The words of caution were along the lines of "Careful, this could blow up in your face." For many white males, engaging in sensitive discussions related to sexism and racism seems to offer a lot of risk and not much reward. The expectation is that well-meaning comments intended to share honest viewpoints might, at best, offend people and, at worst, cause irreparable harm to careers and livelihoods. There are plenty of examples of white people who have made stupid comments and lost their jobs or destroyed their reputation. So why take that risk?

Beverly Daniel Tatum addresses this point in her book *Why Are All the Black Kids Sitting Together in the Cafeteria?* She notes that discussions about race make white people very uncomfortable because they feel they are not as knowledgeable on the topic as people of color and their comments are likely to be misinterpreted.[7] But in fact, it is rarely the case that people trying to genuinely engage in constructive conversation are punished. And we need to create those opportunities for safe conversation so all participants can share their thoughts or ask questions without a fear of recrimination for their ignorance or clumsiness.

In addition to the messages of caution, Michael also received quizzical looks and words of hesitation. People's underlying question was clear: What useful things does a middle-class, heterosexual, able-bodied, cisgender white engineer and son of privilege possibly have to contribute to the topic of diversity, equity, and inclusion? Everyone has been stereotyped and this can cause us to question our involvement and actions. A Latin American man aspiring to be an elected official might have once heard, "Who does a Latino think he is, pretending he can be a political leader?" A woman aspiring to be a doctor before medical schools allowed her to enroll might have heard, "Why does a woman think it is appropriate to study medicine?" It's as if society has constructed false barriers to define who gets to be doctors, lawyers, or any other profession, adopted them as the rule, then rigidly applied the made-up rules to maintain a certain order. We should eliminate false barriers. And in that spirit, white people in positions of power must be a part of the conversation on diversity, equity, and inclusion alongside historically marginalized groups.

In addition, many white people may feel they are not racially biased* and aren't hurt by racism, so they shy away from engaging. That may be because of indifference, an expectation that they have nothing productive to contribute, or fear they might say or do the wrong thing.

While discrimination clearly inflicts direct damage on its targets, it also indirectly affects white people because inhibiting the human potential for anyone takes a toll on society as a whole. It increases the levels of pain felt by its citizens, reduces the total economic activity, and leads to other problems, such as elevated fear, alienation, or violence. That means white people have a stake in solving the problem too, and they must actively engage if we are to see any meaningful progress as a society.

The Goal Is Understanding, Not Just Idle Chatter

The key here is to genuinely understand, not just listen. Michael's experience in graduate school as he pursued his Ph.D. was a challenge. As an undergraduate student at the University of Texas, he was one of the top students in the aerospace engineering department, but in

---

* Readers interested in exploring their own biases might consider taking the Implicit Association Test created by Harvard University. Its results can be eye-opening. https://implicit.harvard.edu/implicit/takeatest.html

graduate school, he was suddenly surrounded by other top students from the best universities around the world. The course load was heavier, and the concepts were more difficult to master. Detailed course notes, extensive homework problems, and many hours of additional studying were required, yet his performance often lagged behind his classmates'. By contrast, it seemed the other students understood the professor's lectures as they were recited and achieved higher marks on exams despite investing much less effort.

After three academic quarters of this grueling experience, a group of 10 graduate students prepared for the daunting qualifying exams, which were a gateway to becoming a candidate in the Ph.D. program. These tests consisted of four 30-minute oral exams conducted in front of a small panel of professors who would pose difficult problems then grill the student as he or she solved it at the whiteboard. The experience is notoriously terrifying, and students have been known to forget simple math or even their own names due to their nerves. Because of the difficulty and high standards of these exams, most students invested in an intense study period of about six weeks over the summer to prepare. Since Michael knew he was behind the other students in terms of his level of mastery for the subjects, he set aside 10 weeks to prepare for the exams. By the time the qualifying exams were complete, only two of the ten students passed all the exams without any conditions. He was one of them.

How did Michael go from a laggard in the class to a top performer? Part of the answer is he simply worked very hard at it, studying for more weeks and longer hours than his peers. His sustained effort was critical. But there is another piece to the story. After more than 20 years in school by that point, and despite being a top student, he had concluded he was simply a slow learner. He also concluded that, fortunately, he was also a slow unlearner. That is, it would take him a while to master a topic, but once he mastered it, it would not be easily forgotten. For years after that, he would tell people he was a slow learner but thankfully had a good memory.

But that's still not the entire story. Somewhere along the way while preparing for his qualifying exams, Michael quit trying to know a subject by learning as much as he could about it and instead focused on *understanding* it. It's easy to memorize many facts, figures, and equations, but it's also very easy to forget them. By contrast, once a person *understands* something, it's very hard to un-understand it. Understanding is the key to mastering any subject. Once a person understands that the force of gravity causes leaves to fall from the trees to the ground and not the other way around, it's hard to imagine not understanding it. People might forget the Pythagorean Theorem, but do they ever forget which way gravity works, thinking leaves jump from the ground to the branches? They don't because they have such a firm intuitive and observational understanding of gravity's forces.

When Michael switched his mode of learning from knowledge to understanding, from memorizing pages of equations or data points to deeply understanding the underlying fundamentals, success was a much likelier outcome. It's easy to forget equations or numbers, but once the reality of the situation is understood, it's hard to go back to not understanding how those forces operate. The same is true with the human experience. Once a person has achieved understanding, it is hard to unlearn the motivational forces that drive our actions. And that is what the goal should be for discussions about diversity, equity, and inclusion. The goal is not to master certain facts and statistics regarding the injustices and costs of racism; rather, the goal should be to understand the different drivers, experiences, emotions, and outcomes of these inequities and work to eliminate them through sustained effort. Instead of simply seeking to learn about diversity, equity, and inclusion—though that is better than nothing—more progress can be made with genuine understanding.

How to Talk About It

When talking about sensitive topics, it is important that the intent and approach are honest and open. Many white people are afraid to discuss race because they are worried they will say something offensive, even if they mean well. They may also feel they have less knowledge and expertise on the subject compared to the life experiences gleaned by people of color. Though valid, this fear inhibits an eagerness to engage. Silence might be more comfortable, but ultimately, silence in the face of discrimination is expensive for society and propagates the problem. As author and Holocaust survivor Elie Wiesel observed during his acceptance speech for the Nobel Prize, "Silence encourages the tormentor, never the tormented."[8]

Members of marginalized groups may unfortunately have more direct experiences to share, but that doesn't mean it is easy for them to discuss these topics. They might worry about how they will be perceived or that they will lose friendships or career opportunities. Others might think that if underrepresented groups are not willing to speak for themselves, who will? Unfortunately, that expectation puts the burden on marginalized groups to always speak up, which can be exhausting and does not always work.

The intent and approach to engagement also matters, especially by members of the power structure. Unfortunately, it is all too common for white people to disrespectfully engage in these conversations or spout false statistics as if they are law or justifications for a lack of concern. Typical examples are when white people say something along the lines of, "Why should we care about high rates of incarceration of Black men when there is so much Black-on-Black violence?" Or when men say, "Why should we care that women are paid less than men? After all, women often choose to leave the workforce to have children, so they deserve it." Though "actively engaged" in the conversation, these statistics or aggressive tactics are often used to justify today's situation or stall the conversation, which does not help further progress.

Though issues of civil rights have been politicized for decades, these conversations need to take place in our daily spaces at home, at work, and in our community. In Stephen Covey's influential book *The 7 Habits of Highly Effective People*, he recommends first seeking to understand before seeking to be understood. This advice is useful not just for effectiveness in business but as a mindset for diversity, equity, and inclusion. The Greek stoic philosopher Epictetus said, "We have two ears and one mouth so that we can listen twice as much as we speak."[9] This captures the essence of these conversations perfectly.

Honest, genuine questioning rather than an interrogation or cross-examination can lead to greater understanding, and as we've just discussed, understanding is the key enabler for achieving greater diversity, equity, and inclusion for all. In addition, here are a few guiding principles to keep in mind:

- Be fully present. Do not focus on past grievances or future problems but listen closely to the words that are being shared in the moment.

- Don't listen to agree; listen to understand. Good communication is not just about how well we speak but how well we listen.

- Don't speak to convince; speak to share. The point of these conversations is not to score points or win the argument.

- Be curious. Ask questions to deepen learning. We all need to be students of this topic.

Importantly, everyone in the conversation should feel free to accept or reject what is said. These conversations are for sharing ideas, not issuing rigid dogma or convincing others of who is right.

How to Facilitate Honest and Open Conversation

Cameron Yarbrough, an executive coach and interpersonal dynamics facilitator at Stanford Graduate School of Business and CEO of Torch, a leadership development start-up, shared an anecdote on social media:

"Yesterday a junior employee reached out to me to give some negative feedback about a decision I made. Inside, I was celebrating. When a junior employee feels psychologically safe enough to give the CEO negative feedback, you know you've built a healthy culture."[10]

When asked how he created that culture at his company, he replied,

"We are explicit about wanting a high feedback culture and have built it into our values. ... Everyone develops the muscles for giving and receiving feedback. Learning how to give critical feedback skillfully requires practice."[11]

Frankly, it is good for all organizations, businesses, and communities to develop and foster a culture of openness and honesty. Plus, in this anecdote, Yarbrough's company practices the art of giving (and receiving) feedback in a safe environment so when the opportunity arises, everyone knows how to give (and receive) it effectively. This openness and trust are necessary preconditions for success with diversity, equity, and inclusion, but also preconditions for sustained success for most meaningful purposes.

Honest feedback is also an integral component of elite athletics. For players and coaches, continual feedback is used to elevate performance. In particular, video footage is a tool used by coaches and teams at all levels and in all sports to improve performance from day to day. Coaches in the professional ranks film their players during every drill in practice and during each game, then they watch the film with them the next workday. The team as a whole and each player's every move is filmed from various angles and can be viewed in slow motion to enlighten the player with one purpose: talk about how that player and/or the team can improve their performance.

Many of the conversations between coaches and players in these film sessions can be difficult, depending on how the player views the intention behind their action. After all, the coach is showing highly skilled athletes all the things they did wrong. But what makes elite professional athletes great is their willingness to look at the film and talk about ways they can improve their play from day to day. The coach's willingness to give critical feedback and the player's willingness to receive it are key ingredients for improvement. Players have an old saying when referencing the video cameras that look down at the field: "The eye in the sky does not lie." Players know what the coach is telling them is the truth because they can clearly see it on the film.

One way the national conversation around social injustice has changed in recent history is through the prevalence of smartphone videos and police body cameras. Just as athletes can use video footage to critique their actions, these viral videos can highlight instances of unfair treatment in society and opportunities for improvement. While we do not recommend recording every hallway exchange or water cooler conversation in an attempt to deliberately capture injustices, we do believe specific feedback and the desire to improve are helpful.

Ultimately, conversation is a key ingredient for affirming personal bonds between teammates and community members. But we cannot just talk: We need to listen and understand. That means we need to be intentional about hearing what is said and be open to feedback about how we can improve.

CHAPTER 4

Check Your Biases and Blind Spots

One of the challenges of working toward justice is identifying and rectifying our biases and blind spots. And the conversations discussed in the prior chapter are good ways for us to learn about our own biases and blind spots. We were not born with our biases and blind spots; we developed them from our worldview, our life experiences, and the way we have been conditioned to think. We carry them out in our lives in the form of our beliefs, habits, attitudes, and expectations. The first step in checking our biases and blind spots is recognizing that we all have them. The next steps are understanding how we gained them and taking action to assure they do not negatively impact others or hinder our ability to achieve our goals in life.

Bias is the contrasting weight we place in favor of or against someone or something we are evaluating. It is a preconceived opinion we hold that affects our conclusions or actions, and it can be favorable or unfavorable. The term "blind spot" may conjure up images of us driving cars. These blind spots are areas around our vehicle that we cannot see with our mirrors. When driving, it is important for us to know where our blind spots are and how to check them to avoid automobile accidents. Have you ever been in a situation in life where, for whatever reason, you were not able to see what was right in front of you? Well, just like the blind spots we deal with while driving, we have blind spots in our everyday lives as well.

When you have a blind spot, it means you are unable to understand or see something properly, although you may be looking right at it. Or if you can see something properly, perhaps you can't see it in its entirety or accurately. For example, you might see an elephant's tail properly without realizing it's attached to a whole elephant. They occur when our thoughts and emotions prevent us from seeing what is right before us.

Just as using a side mirror while driving gives us a fresh perspective in search of obstacles that may hinder our car's path, gathering feedback in life from different perspectives allows us to make progress.

Words Matter

One way to get feedback about biases and blind spots is to be mindful of the body language and facial expressions of the people we communicate with. The responses of others when something insensitive or prejudiced is stated can serve as an immediate gut check to determine if we are off track. Michael misfires with his words much more often than he likes to admit, and that real-time feedback helps him to correct his course.

This also means that if your world is composed of homogeneity and echo chambers, you aren't likely to get honest feedback because the person you are communicating with might not notice your offensive words either. Just like a driver needs multiple mirrors to gain access to suitable perspectives, we must broaden our perspectives by building diverse social and professional circles. This is a point Michael discussed firsthand with a friend, who is a suburban schoolteacher. She shared that she is in three separate all-white book clubs that are all reading books about racism. They both laughed at the ridiculousness of it. Reading about racism in an all-white book club is better than nothing, but it might not move the needle as much as diversifying the book clubs themselves would.

Furthermore, feedback from others only works if people are able to communicate freely and openly without masking what they feel. If they cannot speak freely, then inappropriate comments might be met with silence or stone-faced expressions that send an incorrect signal of tacit approval.

For professors working with students, facilitating free and open communication is especially relevant because the relationship is so asymmetric. The power dynamic is uneven, as students usually feel the professor holds power over their grades, academic progress, and future career. In those situations, it is difficult for students to feel that they can speak freely for fear of offending someone they perceive to hold a unique power over them. So Michael works hard in his classes and with his research group to foster an accepting attitude by explicitly asking for feedback and signaling that he is ready to accept it. Doing so pays off because he is able to get honest feedback from students, which improves his effectiveness as a teacher.

In the world of electronics, there is a famous relationship between voltage (symbolized with a V), current (symbolized with an I), and resistance (symbolized with an R). The relationship is $V=IR$ (the voltage is equal to the current multiplied by the resistance). For decades, to remember the terms, electronics handbooks used the memory trick "vultures fly over Indians and rabbits," noting that vultures fly in the air and therefore are above Indians and rabbits that walk on the ground. Michael used this memory trick in class lectures and for an online textbook until a student noted that the trick was, at best, dated ("Indians" is a dated and Euro-centric term for Native Americans) and, at worst, harmful or offensive (as it implies Indians are on par with animals or fit for carrion).

Michael had never even thought about the memory trick's hidden messages, but of course, his students were right. He was not trying to say anything offensive, but nevertheless was propagating potentially offensive terminology without stopping to think about it. His students would not have alerted him if they did not feel he was open to input. Changing the memory trick to "vultures fly over *iguanas* and rabbits" made the exact same point without any reference to race. And generally speaking, we should examine our language for *any* references to race, ethnicity, gender, and so forth and ask ourselves whether it's necessary or if it can be replaced.

Mindlessly propagating race-laden terminology is one example of a blind spot that needs fixing, but there are other things that are harmful, either because they reflect prejudice or propagate stereotypes. The damage can be significant, even if the propagator does not have malevolent intent. Michael can confess to two other examples from his experience to illustrate.

During the summer between his senior year of high school and freshman year of college, he needed to earn money quickly to pay his way through the upcoming semesters, and the more he could save up before classes started, the easier it would be once he got to school. He was 18 years old at the time and, with one of his best friends who was in a similar predicament, decided to open a lawn-mowing business, as they both liked to be outside and work with their hands. Plus, lawn mowing was lucrative. They took the money they had saved washing dishes at the local barbecue restaurant and invested in a high-end mower and trimmer, printed up flyers, then proceeded to knock on doors to advertise their new business. They decided to focus on the rich parts of town to maximize the prospects for high fees.

They split up and took different sides of the street, starting in Tarrytown, an affluent neighborhood in central Austin with many doctors, lawyers, and state representatives as residents. Michael spotted one particular house with a nice yard and knocked on the door. An older Black woman with dark clothes and a nice apron opened the door. Michael eagerly told her with pride and enthusiasm about how he was mowing lawns to pay his way through college as she listened politely. He closed his sales pitch by asking her if she would be so kind as to pass the flyer onto the homeowner. As he heard the words leave his lips and saw her facial expression fall, he realized what he had said was horribly prejudiced.

He had assumed that because she was Black and in a nice neighborhood, she was the housekeeper or cook and not the homeowner. Who was he to draw such conclusions? He was clearly the perpetrator of racial prejudice, and though he immediately realized what he had done and remembers it clear as day even decades later, by then it was too late to take it back; the damage was done. How do you think his words made her feel? Did she feel uplifted and encouraged, or might she have been disappointed and put down? Perhaps these kinds of racial microaggressions were a common feature in her life, and no doubt Michael has made many other similar trespasses without realizing or remembering them.

Another example comes from his teenage years, but this time, he did not recognize the potential harm from his actions until years later. When he was in high school, Michael would write letters from Texas to a friend who attended boarding school in New England. The letters normally included the usual shallow teenage banter, but in one letter, as a fun exercise, he made a mock-up of what a college application for an Asian American student would look like compared to an application of a white person. He assumed for this fake college application that the Asian American student was excellent at academics and would certainly be admitted, so the application was short: a list of grades, SAT score, and the musical instruments the fake student had mastered. No need for long essays or other expressions of merit.

While this bigotry propagated a positive stereotype—the idea that all Asian Americans were excellent students—it is damaging nevertheless. First of all, it presents the caricature that all Asians have mastered a musical instrument, with violin and piano as the stereotypical options. That certainly isn't true and plays into racist tropes of overbearing Asian parents forcing their children to practice their music every day. More important, his mockery revealed his participation in broader white resentment and a fear that Asian Americans were taking over all the spots at good schools that rightfully belonged to white students. In fact, many white people opposed affirmative action for minorities they perceived to be less deserving (e.g., Blacks and Hispanic Americans) but have sought affirmative action for themselves to reserve spots at competitive schools they feel have been unfairly allocated to Asian American students. Lawsuits against selective high schools in San Francisco or Ivy League universities for admitting too many Asian Americans and not enough white people drive this point home. Although not a negative stereotype in the vein of "people of color just want handouts," the positive stereotype of Asian Americans being high performers because all they do is work also can be damaging.

Michael did not recognize this form of racial prejudice until several years later. An article was published in the university paper in his early 20s that shifted his thinking. The article discussed rising incidences of anti-Asian hate speech and bigotry on campus. In particular, it talked about the aggression Asian American students experienced because students from other races were afraid they would outperform everyone in class. It was not unusual for students to whisper, "Here comes the curve-busters," when Asian American students took their seats in class. The implication was clear: Asian Americans would earn the top scores in class and ruin the grading curve for others.

This stereotype can still be harmful for everyone affected. If indeed Asian American students perform well, it won't be perceived to have been from their hard work and discipline but, rather, their race. The white, Black, Hispanic, and Native American students in the room who didn't earn the top score might grouse that it was because of their own race, namely that they were *not* Asian, that prevented them from achieving at such a high level (rather than their study habits or talent). If the Asian American student doesn't earn the top score, it could be perceived by other students and even teachers more negatively—as more of a disappointment—than what the other students might experience if they earned a similar score. So the Asian American students are caught in a web of expectations imposed by others simply because of their race.

The article in the student newspaper caught Michael's eye. He asked an Asian American student in one of his classes about the article, and that student confirmed that he had heard similar grumbling when he walked into class on the first day. It's as if the class collectively groans, "Oh, no. There's an Asian in this class. That means we will actually have to do our work to keep up."

There are other positive prejudices that can be harmful. It might feel like you are paying a compliment to someone by saying they look very young, but in academia and medicine, that can be problematic. Young researchers and doctors and nurses are not taken as seriously as older ones. This is particularly a problem for young-looking women. By saying, "You look young," the professor or medical professional you intend to compliment might hear, "You look like you don't know what you're talking about." In the world of scientific research, not knowing what you are talking about is the kiss of death for the reputations of scholars.

Stereotypes are propagated with books, movies, TV shows, and other popular cultural references, making the situation feel intractable. One lesson is that both negative and positive stereotypes also inflict damage, so we should drop them entirely. As Dr. King advised, we should judge people by the content of their characters and not the color of their skin. For Michael, his school's newspaper article was helpful in illuminating his prejudice and the damage it can cause. The example shows that a little awareness can go a long way in helping us make progress.

Keep in mind that words matter. The words we choose make an impact, and we have to be mindful not to use those words to typecast people or propagate stereotypes. For example, we should not use our words to discourage girls from pursuing math or boys from being caring. Systemic bias is not our fault; it is something we inherited, but that doesn't mean we can't take steps to correct it. As a professor, Michael knows how hard it is for students to admit mistakes. Rather than admitting a mistake, learning from it, and moving on, some students will keep arguing their point. It's kind of like how people have trouble switching who they vote for from one election to the next because doing so would admit that they were wrong the first time. But admitting our mistakes is a great way to learn from them.

Early in Johnnie's school years, he struggled in math. That all changed when he took Mrs. Mayer's algebra class at La Grange High School. Johnnie credits her for being one of the people who put him in a position to achieve his goals in life. Prior to taking Mrs. Mayer's class, Johnnie had heard many negative things about her. The word around school was that "you better hope you don't get Mrs. Mayer because she's such a hard teacher." So when he was placed in her class, he did not feel like he belonged. That was until one day after Mrs. Mayer saw Johnnie walking down the hallway at school before his first day in her class. She informed him that she would like to speak with him.

As he nervously walked into her classroom and politely said hello, she looked at him and said, "Johnnie, I understand you are a really good football player," to which he barely responded. All he could think about were the comments he had heard around school about how hard of a teacher she was. She went on to say, "I want you to know that I expect you to give me the same level of commitment and effort in my class that you give your coaches on the football field." What a relief! She was simply holding him to a high standard, the same high standard as his coaches. Johnnie not only gave great effort on the football field, he was passionately committed to playing the game. He had a strong belief that he belonged there.

Mrs. Mayer was a demanding teacher. She assigned homework every day, and on some days, every student in the class had to answer one of the questions on the homework from the prior night out loud to the rest of the class. If one of Johnnie's classmates gave an incorrect answer, he became one of two students called upon to give the correct answer. Despite his initial biases toward the class and Mrs. Mayer, he went on to earn an A in algebra that year. He discovered, through Mrs. Mayer's teachings, that he had a blind spot when it came to math, and with her assistance, he was able to change his way of thinking and overcome it. Unbeknownst to Johnnie at the time, he had taken a step toward achieving one of his goals. Algebra was one of the core subjects he needed to pass to qualify for college admission.

Privilege Can Lead to Blind Spots

In addition to checking our biases, it is also helpful to recognize our privilege and how that might create blind spots that limit our effectiveness when engaging with others.

Growing up, Michael never thought about privilege or racism. Because he grew up in a rich neighborhood but was a professor's child, he actually felt poor. His friends went on fancier vacations and drove nicer cars. His car in high school didn't have a radio or air conditioning, which made for hot and boring drives in the Texas sun. Other parents hired maids and the mothers cooked for the children. By contrast, in Michael's house, each child had to do their own chores and make their own school lunches starting at age 6. Over the course of 12 years of schooling, Michael's mother packed his school lunch exactly once. It was in the third grade, and he remembers it to this day because it was such a unique experience.

His friends' parents gave them spending money, but if Michael wanted to go to a movie or the arcade, he had to earn the money himself. As a result, he started doing odd jobs in junior high and worked in restaurants as a dishwasher or busboy throughout high school. Because of the collapsed oil market and failed real estate market in Texas in the mid-1980s, his parents even went bankrupt during his junior year in high school, so for a while, he had to buy his own clothes. If you had asked Michael as a teenager about his privilege, he would have reeled off a list of injustices he had suffered compared to those around him.

In fact, as the son of a professor, he lived a privileged life. His father's job was stable, so the family was never at risk of going hungry. His father even took sabbaticals to Europe when Michael was 12 and 15, so he had the opportunity to live in Switzerland and Paris. This sounds fairly exotic. And it was. As a white male, the educational system and local power structures were tilted in his favor. He had no idea how sheltered his life was until his high school girlfriend pointed it out. She had been to poorer schools and recognized how rich theirs was. She also recognized the lack of diversity; the school was almost entirely white when Michael graduated in 1989.

Michael's experience growing up as a white male was different from what other genders or races experienced. As a consequence, there were naturally going to be blind spots that hindered his ability to genuinely understand others.

A more recent example illustrates Michael's privilege well: In 2018, Michael was selected to participate in a distinguished leadership development program organized by Presidents George W. Bush and Bill Clinton. This unique program was built with diversity in mind, primarily political diversity, with the goal of bringing Republicans, Democrats, conservatives, and liberals together. But it also had gender, racial, and geographic diversity, drawing people from different backgrounds and states. Hundreds of people typically apply for the program each year, and only 60 are allowed to participate. Michael was honored and thrilled to work with the presidents and their staffs over the course of six months. The training program took place at their two presidential libraries and also at the libraries for Presidents George H.W. Bush and Lyndon Johnson.

During one particularly difficult group conversation about a contentious policy issue, Michael suggested that perhaps it would make sense to work with municipal police departments to serve as a trusted facilitator of dialogue. Every Black person in the room snapped their heads around to him like he was crazy. After a momentary silence, one Black member of the leadership cohort politely told Michael that the police aren't always trusted in the Black community. How could Michael have not seen this after Spike Lee's 1989 movie *Do the*

Right Thing examined trust between Blacks and city police, after the release of the videotaped police beatings of Rodney King, the protests in Ferguson, Missouri, over the killing of Michael Brown by a white police officer, and after countless other Black deaths at the hands of the police? After all those headlines, protests, and other opportunities to learn over several decades, Michael was *still* blind to the possibility that trust in police might vary from one group to another based on the differences in their experience.

This was a blind spot born out of his privilege. When white men are pulled over by police, they have a very different level of fear from what a Black man might feel when he is pulled over. Michael's niece is married to a Black man, and when he gets pulled over—and he gets pulled over more often than she does—he calls her and puts his phone on speaker so she can listen in case anything goes wrong. By contrast, it had never occurred to Michael that this might be necessary.

And of course there are other blind spots or advantages that flow from our upbringing, so we have to remain alert to how our background limits our perspective. Blind spots are often born out of privilege. Privilege refers to the often invisible, unacknowledged benefits granted to a particular person or group of people through no virtue of their own, but these benefits are made to look normal and available to any person who wants them. Male privilege addresses not so much what men have but what they don't need to think about and/or negotiate on a daily basis. White privilege refers to the advantages available to white people that people of color cannot readily enjoy. These advantages might feel subtle or quiet to its beneficiaries but might not be so subtle or quiet to those who are marginalized.

To be clear, many whites grow up in poverty or other adverse conditions. So the concept of white privilege is not that every white person has an easy upbringing. Rather, the point is that no matter the situation, whiteness offers some advantage. Growing up as a poor, white person can be difficult, but growing up as a poor, Black person adds additional difficulties beyond what the poor white person endures. Privilege is usually not the result of direct malicious action but, rather, a systemic collection of passive beneficial actions and decisions. The cumulative damage, whether known or unknown, is significant.

And to be even more clear, white privilege isn't the only form of privilege. There is also economic privilege, urban privilege, and celebrity privilege. A case can even be made that today, there are biases against white football players playing defensive back, especially at the collegiate and pro levels. Johnnie observed the position transform from one played by mostly white players to one consisting of predominantly Black players during his active playing career.

At each level, the defensive unit is made up of three groups: defensive linemen, linebackers, and defensive backs. In the defensive backfield, where Johnnie specialized in college and the NFL, the base starting unit is made up of four players: two cornerbacks and two safeties. There are circumstances when a defensive coordinator will switch from a base defense to what is called a nickel, dime, or dollar defensive set. This is when additional defensive backs are inserted to join the four already on the field for a combined five, six, or seven total players among that position group. This modification occurs most often when the offensive team is in situations where they are most likely to throw a forward pass. Today, even when there are seven defensive backs on the field, it is rare that any of them will be white.

On their 1975 Texas state championship team, Johnnie's three other starting defensive backfield teammates were all white. This was not unusual at the high school level during this era since the integration of public schools and Black players in sports really did not start to take shape until the mid-1960s. When Johnnie arrived at the University of Texas as a freshman in 1976, he became a starter in the defensive backfield. As a senior in college, he played alongside one white and two Black teammates. When Johnnie arrived in the NFL, he again started alongside one white and two Black teammates; however, during the latter part of his NFL career with the Rams, all of the defensive backs among his group were Black. When you look around the NFL today, it is not uncommon for the majority, if not the entire defensive backfield group, to be all Black or people of color.

Think about that: In the span of just one or two decades, professional football went from barely integrated with a few Black players here and there to almost completely Black in the defensive backfield. There are many ways to look at what has occurred here, but one of the first revolves around why more white players are being overlooked when it comes to having an opportunity to play this position at the collegiate and NFL levels. And it's not because of a lack of talent. In the youth leagues and high school levels, there are certainly qualified white candidates playing these positions, but over time they either switch positions or sports. Is this the result of an unfair bias against white players and for Black players at this position? Successful defensive backs need to be fast and agile —do coaches subconsciously feel that Blacks naturally have these qualities or that whites lack these qualities?

It starts with the preconceptions held by decision-makers who choose the candidates. This is not intentional; it is merely the way the decision-makers have been conditioned to think and view the world.

Decision-makers in the business world hold preconceptions as well. This worldview may lead to a white executive experiencing some form of privilege while moving up the ladder in corporate America then hiring other white people to join his or her team once they get to the top. Meanwhile, people of color may face some degree of discrimination when they seek to take the same steps. In both sports and corporate arenas, qualified candidates are ready and waiting for the opportunity to perform. In either case, white defensive backs and minority executives face an uphill battle in their fight for inclusion.

We must all work to level the playing field and support diversity, equity, and inclusion for all, whether it be in sports, corporate America, or our community. Part of the process involves reminding ourselves that we all have biases and blind spots and correcting ourselves if we become aware of unintentionally choosing people based on how they look. We also have a responsibility to alert our colleagues if they act on their blind spots. The latter is an important step because it is often difficult for us to see where we are going wrong, so we might need others to point it out to us.

Ultimately, we all have some biases, blind spots, and privileges. The fact you are reading this book is a statement of privilege, as there are a billion-plus people living in poverty worldwide who do not have access to books in printed, electronic, or audio formats. We need to recognize and appreciate our privilege and then identify and rectify our biases. One way to reduce the effect of prejudice is to increase contact between groups. As diversity expert Lauren Leader-Chivée explains in her book *Crossing the Thinnest Line*,[12] if the contact between equal-status minority and majority groups is increased in the pursuit of common goals, then prejudice can be reduced. In other words, much of prejudice stems from ignorance or a lack of contact between groups. But bringing those groups together on equal footing, as fellow players in a sport or new recruits at a company, increases contact, enhances awareness, diminishes ignorance, and reduces prejudice. It is important to note that this effect can be amplified through institutional support.

CHAPTER 5

Expand Your Comfort Zone

Most people do not want to engage in uncomfortable conversations—quite the opposite in fact; most people seek to avoid them. If sensitive subjects *do* come up, they can induce an awkwardness and silence, causing many to quickly change the subject. But if we keep changing the subject or avoiding the topic, we won't make the progress we need to make, so it's important that we expand our comfort zones.

Have you ever wondered why you sometimes feel at home in certain situations and uptight, tense, and uncomfortable in others? Usually, when we are tense and uptight, we're doing something outside of our comfort zone. Our comfort zone is where we feel comfortable, and it is regulated by our self-image. If we see ourselves as confident and able to adapt to certain situations, our comfort zone will be far-reaching. If our dominant self-image is one of self-doubt and inferiority, we will have a more confining comfort zone. When we operate in our comfort zone, we are often able to be productive and perform with confidence, but trying to operate outside of it often leaves us unable to consistently utilize our full potential, causing our performance to suffer. This is why expanding our comfort zone is essential for growth. Growing is essentially the process of expanding the range where we can perform both comfortably and at a high level.

In the world of athletics, it's captured in student athletes' transition from high school to college in a matter of a few months. One day, they are playing their respective sport against other high school athletes as one of the star players on their team, possibly even in their state, and are confident each time they head into competition. Then, they graduate high school and head off to college where they find themselves competing against many other elite athletes. Student athletes must adjust by expanding their comfort zone and utilizing more of their full potential at the collegiate level; otherwise they might not succeed.

There are several other ways that student athletes must adjust when they arrive to college. They must become comfortable with being away from home; they must adjust to the new classroom environment; and they must find their way socially in a highly competitive and diverse environment. Student athletes will need to expand their comfort zone in all of these areas to give themselves the opportunity to use more of their potential and achieve their goals at the collegiate level. The process is not easy. The same is true for building trust and collaborating with your family and colleagues in the pursuit of diversity, equity, and inclusion for all.

Imposter Syndrome

Have you ever felt nervous that people would find out you did not know the information in your presentation as well as you thought you should have? Have you ever spoken in front of an audience and were afraid someone would find out that you don't really know what you're talking about? Have you ever played sports in front of a crowd and worried you would make a mistake? If so, you might have experienced a phenomenon called "imposter syndrome." Imposter syndrome is the experience of worrying that you are not as competent in your role as you think you should be, and it's something Michael experiences on a regular basis.

Interestingly, imposter syndrome is especially prevalent among professors. Their jobs are to be experts in their fields, yet they often experience a perpetual sense of dread that everyone will discover they are not as smart as advertised. For example: One of Michael's colleagues in the mechanical engineering department was one of the world's leading experts in his field of study. He literally wrote the book—multiple books, actually—on his core expertise. When Michael was a new professor, he sought him out as a mentor and asked the older professor about imposter syndrome. This distinguished professor said it never goes away. Though he was in his 70s and had been honored many times with awards, including selection for the elite National Academy of Engineering—a distinguished body for which membership is reserved only for the most highly regarded engineers in the nation—he shared a surprising insight: The feeling of not being as good as people think you are never leaves. That was a jaw-dropping moment. If the best of the best experience imposter syndrome, then what is a lowly junior faculty member supposed to do?

This distinguished professor, as well as other faculty colleagues in subsequent mentoring sessions, pointed out that imposter syndrome is not necessarily a bad thing. It can be a sign of humility and the result of learning something new and pushing the envelope. For context, professors have one of the best jobs in the world, as they are paid to learn their entire lives. And to learn new subjects, they must expand their comfort zone beyond the topics they have already mastered. Expanding the comfort zone and learning are two descriptions of the same phenomenon. From this perspective, imposter syndrome is the result of plowing new intellectual ground.

Professors do not feel imposter syndrome when they are presenting the same work they have been presenting for decades, which they know inside and out. Instead, they feel it when they are in new territory and aren't as confident. But this humility that accompanies imposter syndrome can be healthy and is much better than arrogance and overconfidence. This same approach should be used for addressing diversity, equity, and inclusion. Rather than having overconfidence and assuming we have all the answers, we should approach the topic with humility.

Athletes also experience imposter syndrome, but there are differences: consistent rules and frequent coaching. In sports, there are clear sets of guidelines and rules that govern the athlete's participation. Coaches work with athletes with one goal in mind: to inspire athletes to be the best they can be at their sport. Athletes are evaluated daily, and the feedback lets them know how they are performing and if their performance is sufficient enough to achieve their goal for the day, whether it be in practice, during a game, or throughout the season.

Like professors, athletes at the pro ranks have one of the best jobs in the world. They are paid handsomely to play a game they love. And no matter how successful they become in their profession, they know critics will be looking for them to make a mistake. And they know they need to keep learning to be a better player. To improve in this matter, they must expand their comfort zone beyond the levels they have already mastered. From this perspective, imposter syndrome is not an unusual result when cultivating new intellectual ground or new skill sets.

Improvement Requires Leaving Your Comfort Zone

Michael's transition from high school to college was a straightforward one with little shock to his sense of social standing. He went to the same university where his father was a professor and where his two older siblings were students. He had practically grown up on that campus, so it was familiar and comfortable. Going to classes there, just a few miles from home with several high school classmates as college roommates in a setting he knew well, made the whole experience easy; it felt like an extension of high school. That was part of his white male privilege, but there was an extra layer of privilege in being a professor's son.

Johnnie's experience was very different. Because he was a star athlete, he had many options for college. He chose to accept a scholarship to play football at the University of Texas at Austin, departing the smalltown La Grange High School for one of the largest universities in the nation. Johnnie had already expanded his comfort zone after school integration took him from his small all-Black school in La Grange, Texas, to the formerly all-white school across town. Switching schools and entering a mixed-race classroom was terrifying. He had to expand his comfort zone to participate in the school's activities and receive his education. The transition to the university was yet another jolt to his system.

The U.S. census for La Grange in 1970 recorded a population of approximately 3,100 people. One dorm at the University of Texas campus, Jester Center, housed around 3,100 students. Think about that: Johnnie's entire hometown could fit in a single dormitory building on campus. He was aware of only four Black professors on the faculty at the time, and the few Black students enrolled were, for the most part, athletes. Johnnie's parents did not go to college, so he did not have their experiences to guide him in the transition. For Johnnie, it was a whole different world. He had to expand his comfort zone to survive and thrive in his new social setting, which had different rules and rhythms from what he experienced as a child.

Beyond their social adjustments to collegiate life, there were also requirements to excel in the classroom and on the field. While Michael's social adjustment was seamless, his classroom performance initially floundered, and while Johnnie's social adjustment was more difficult, his athletic performance flourished. How could this be?

Michael was a star student at his high school, which is considered one of the best high schools in the nation. He was one of the top-ranked students out of the 398 members of his graduating class, despite the fact he worked several nights each week as a busboy and dishwasher at a local barbecue restaurant in addition to serving in leadership roles at school. He even earned his school's Calculus Award, given to the best math student in the senior class. Unfortunately, he did not develop good study habits, did not complete his homework or class projects with much enthusiasm or dedication, and was not serious about studying before exams. While he could get away with that in high school, that same approach of cramming for exams the night before, blowing off class projects until the last minute, and not completing his homework in a timely manner was not a successful strategy at the university level.

All of a sudden, Michael was surrounded by other star students from other high schools around the world. Though top scores came readily and consistently in high school, in college that same lazy approach yielded much lower grades. This was new territory for Michael. He was out of his comfort zone and he had to develop a new approach. He had to expand his comfort zone to deal with the challenge of learning in an academic setting that had much higher expectations. He had to reinvent his approach to class. It wasn't until his junior year that he finally started to develop good study habits and was able to perform in line with his intellectual level.

Just as Michael was surrounded by other star students in the classroom, Johnnie was surrounded by other star athletes on the field. He often describes his transition from La Grange High School to the University of Texas on and off the field as "feeling like the distance between the Earth and the moon." It was a culture shock to his system. Johnnie struggled in the classroom when he first arrived on campus, where one lecture hall sat nearly as many students as his entire high school in La Grange. His struggles were more about him being out of his comfort zone in the classroom; by contrast, there was one place where Johnnie felt comfortable, and that was when he was around his new teammates in the athletic building and on the practice field. This is where he was able to demonstrate his exceptional training habits early and often. But now that Johnnie was in college, he needed to learn how to expand his comfort zone in all areas of life—in the classroom, on the field, and socially—if he was to have any chance of achieving his childhood goal of playing in the NFL.

Although Johnnie practiced great habits in high school, they were not sufficient once he arrived at the college level. In other words, what worked against high school players would not consistently work against elite diverse college players. He would need to improve. He went on to do just that, becoming an All-American in college and number one pick of the Los Angeles Rams in the 1980 NFL draft.

If his transition from high school to college was like the difference between the Earth and the moon, the transition from Austin, Texas, to Los Angeles, California, was like going from the Earth to Mars. As a result, he was way out of his comfort zone again in just about everything he did except under one circumstance: when he was around his new teammates doing football-related activities, such as attending practice and meetings. But that comfort didn't last long because he needed to learn the Rams' new system, adjust to the talent around the NFL, and adjust to life as a professional football player living in the community.

Furthermore, although Johnnie was at the top of his game in college, his skills were not sufficient for professional football. In other words, what worked against elite college players would not work against the highly experienced and diverse veterans in the NFL. Once again, he needed to take his game to the next level.

When he was drafted, Johnnie set a goal to play in the NFL for 10 years. The average NFL career at that time was three-and-a-half years. To meet his goal, one of the first things Johnnie did when he arrived at the Rams was identify the players who had been in the league for eight years or longer and learn everything he could about them. He wanted to know their study and practice regimens, so that he could pattern his habits in those areas after those legends of the game. He learned that many of the habits he had practiced to become a first-round draft pick were similar to the ones that the veterans practiced daily. The difference was that he had not done it at the NFL level while facing all the new obstacles, barriers, or twists and turns that can potentially hinder a professional player.

Johnnie realized that it was not just their talent that enabled the veteran athletes to successfully perform as long as they had in the league; it was also their ability to take steps each day to improve their performance, despite circumstances that could potentially drive them away from their goal. If he were to achieve his goal of playing for 10 years, he would need to expand his comfort zone to be able to consistently practice those fundamental activities no matter what.

Just as Michael had to develop new skills and refine his approach to academics to master the transition from high school to college to graduate school, Johnnie had to develop new habits and refine his approach to athletics from high school to college to the professional leagues. If both had not expanded their comfort zones and taken on new challenges, they would have become frozen at their early levels. Becoming elite in any field requires you to constantly push yourself out of your comfort zone, which forces you to grow, learn, and then execute at a higher level.

Basically, expanding your comfort zone involves putting yourself in the best position to use your full potential in everything you do, against any level of competition. And you need to be using your full potential when you are playing in a league full of elite diverse professional athletes and coaches, who as opponents are on a mission to defeat you every time they take the field. Each stage of competition forced Johnnie to expand his comfort zone and elevate his game.

For people who want to improve diversity, equity, and inclusion in their community, expanding comfort zones could mean a few different paths. It could mean looking for different candidates to interview and hire for positions at our companies, recruiting diverse participants for our clubs and organizations, reading a wider range of books and news sources written by diverse authors, and much more. Instead of defaulting to whatever is easiest and most comfortable within our professional and social circles, we should explore different cultures and points of view. For those who can travel, visiting new places is a great way to immerse yourself in something new and gain new insights.

Complacently staying in our comfort zone causes us to passively propagate the status quo, which ultimately hinders our path toward diversity, equity, and inclusion for all. Leaders can set good examples by specifically declaring intentions to diversify and broaden perspectives.

As mentors, supervisors, friends, and colleagues, it's up to us to help others expand their comfort zones as much as we can by removing systemic barriers to access and in some cases, directly providing opportunities to do so.

CHAPTER 6

Build Diverse Teams

If it were easy to jump to this point, we would have recommended building diverse teams as the first and only step, as such teams are one of the primary desired outcomes of the support we recommend. They're also a key input to achieving equity and inclusion. However, building diverse teams often requires that the steps we outlined in prior chapters be implemented first.

Diversity Improves Outcomes

Many people are skeptical that diversity is valuable. However, there is ample evidence that diversity helps companies perform better. Studies by management consultants McKinsey & Company, as well as publications in the Harvard Business Review, report that diversity is a competitive advantage rather than just a courtesy extended out of political correctness or a sense of social obligation. One McKinsey & Company[13] study found that the most diverse companies outperform less diverse companies on key indicators, such as profitability. Further, it concluded that the relationship between diversity and performance has grown over the years. Notably, the study observes that in times of crisis, companies with multiple perspectives are likely to make bolder, better decisions.

One specific write-up in the Harvard Business Review[14] points out that organizations without any women on their boards generated a lower return on equity and lower net income growth than those with at least one female board member. There are different reasons to explain this phenomenon, but it seems that diverse teams are more likely to remain objective when examining facts and processing information more carefully. In the end, heterogenous teams perform with higher collective intelligence and are more innovative than homogenous teams.

For Michael's workplace, the workforce for the main corporate research laboratory in Paris that reports to him is 37 percent women, which is much higher than what is typical in engineering and scientific research labs. They got to that level because the lab recruits for technical excellence rather than for particular gender stereotypes. This diversity is a good sign since according to that same Harvard Business Review piece, a study of thousands of research and development teams showed that companies with more women produced more innovations compared to companies with fewer women.

Diversity Is Much More Than Just Gender or Race

Returning to the football field, it seems clear that successful teams need a combination of skills and capabilities to thrive. The lighter 200-pound defensive backs provide speed and agility, whereas a 300-pound lineman meets the needs for strength and mass. Yet both can provide critical momentum to make a tackle.

That is why the most productive and successful football teams have a well-blended and diverse mix of athletes based on their height, weight, physical strength, and speed. It would be ridiculous for a football team to only include large, strong, slow players or light, fast, agile players. It would also be ridiculous for a basketball team to only include tall players, excluding smaller ball handlers or vice versa. A football team of just heavy players or fast players will not be as competitive as a team with a mix of capabilities, nor would a baseball team with all right-handed or left-handed pitchers or hitters be as competitive as a team with a healthy combination of those players. This is true for engineering teams too.

The football example demonstrates why professional sports organizations are a leader in this area, at least on the playing field. Major professional sports teams started their most visible integration of players in the 1960s—earlier than many other organizations—and have made much broader strides than many industrial sectors. That is a promising sign, but there is still a lack of diversity in the top coaching positions and executive ranks, so the march of progress isn't complete.

While racial and gender diversity are important, there are other parameters to consider. Let us give an example from a university setting. The U.S. Department of Energy organizes an international competition called the Solar Decathlon. The goal of the program is to design and build an energy-efficient house that can operate solely on solar energy from panels on the home's roof or elsewhere on its site. Dozens of teams from around the world that make it to the finals spend more than a year preparing. For one particular competition, Michael served as a faculty advisor for a team of engineering and architecture students in Texas who partnered with students with similar academic disciplines from Germany. The team had excellent gender diversity. Equally important, the team also had a mix of architects (with great skills at producing beautiful design) and engineers (with great skills at producing functional designs). This diversity helped the team pursue a design that was both elegant and innovative while also achieving high utility.

Interestingly, the team really struggled along the way. The German team kept designing a home that would effectively retain heat to manage the Northern European winters, and the Texas team kept designing overhangs to provide shade, reject heat, and keep the house cool during southern summers. Frankly, a good house needs to do both. If the team had just been Texan or German, the house would have been too narrowly designed for one season or another, but because of their international and geographic diversity, they designed a more robust house. The contest had more than 150 entries, the team earned fourth place overall, beating academic heavyweights, such as Yale and Stanford. The team also earned first place in the category specific to energy efficiency. The team's diversity more than paid off: It was a strength.

A lack of diversity in company teams can lead to inferior products and services that fail to address the customers' needs, which therefore achieve lower market success than they would have if the teams were more diverse.

In 2009, in time for the Christmas shopping season, Hewlett-Packard (HP) released a computer with an innovative design that included a camera with automatic face-tracking software. The idea was that with this camera, the user could move around in his or her chair or at a desk while on videoconference calls and the camera would track their face so it remained in frame. In a two-minute YouTube video that has since been viewed millions of times[15], a Black male customer who purchased the new technology demonstrated that the face-tracking software would not follow his face, but it would follow his white female co-worker's face.[16] Ultimately, the engineers designed the system based on particular assumptions about skin tone, light reflection, and shadows. Does this mean HP is a racially prejudiced company? No, but it probably does mean they lacked diversity in their engineering teams for design and debugging. Were dark-skinned engineers part of the team that tested the technology? If so, would this problem have been caught before the product was shipped to market? How many customers were lost and how much damage did the company's reputation suffer because of this problem? A lack of diversity is simply bad for business.

It's not just skin tone diversity that is relevant. After YouTube created an app to facilitate the upload of videos for smartphone users, it discovered that 5 to 10 percent of the videos were uploaded upside down. Why was this? Because it had accidentally designed the app to work for right-handed users only. Many right-handed smartphone users would rotate their phone 90 degrees to capture a video in landscape mode. But left-handed smartphone users would rotate their phone 90 degrees the other direction to capture videos. As a result, landscape videos recorded by left-handed customers were flipped 180 degrees—that is, upside down—compared to those recorded by right-handed customers.[17] Did YouTube intentionally discriminate against left-handed users? No. Rather, the situation is a result of unconscious bias by its almost exclusively right-handed design and test teams. Because its team lacked diversity, it produced a product or service that did not meet the needs of all its customers.

These experiences are instructive because they serve as reminders that diversity means more than just Black/white diversity. There are many factors to consider, including background, place of upbringing, usage patterns, and mindset.

Take a Proactive Role in Building Teams

When Michael first started teaching as a professor, he was assigned a faculty mentor, Phil Schmidt. A legendary instructor who had received just about every major teaching award at the university, Dr. Schmidt had taught every core class in mechanical engineering at one point or another over his multidecade career. It was not unusual for alumni to reach out to him many years after taking his class to thank him for what he had taught them. In thermodynamics, which is a notoriously difficult sophomore course for mechanical engineering students, a section of the semester introduces complex and abstract concepts, such as entropy and the Second Law of Thermodynamics. Instead of going to the chalkboard to start writing out intimidating equations with Greek symbols, he would dress up in period costume with a hat, cape, and cane to represent Sadi Carnot, the French scientist who developed these concepts in the early 1800s. Carnot's book, *Reflections on the Motive Power of Fire,* taught its readers how to turn heat into motion, which is one of the underpinning breakthroughs of the Industrial Revolution.

Dr. Schmidt, in character, would walk slowly into class then surprise his students by using a French accent to slowly tell Carnot's life story and explain the evolution of how he came to understand thermodynamics and entropy. It's not often that engineering professors act like a centuries-old Frenchman, but that's the kind of thing Dr. Schmidt would do so his students would pay attention. They talk about it years later.

Since Michael was assigned to him as his mentee, he had the good fortune to absorb his lessons on how to be an effective instructor, and the best way to learn was to teach side by side so Michael could mimic his approach. For his first few years as a professor, Michael co-taught not only thermodynamics but also an introductory freshman course. During that first-semester freshman course of 20 students, a group project was assigned that required the students to form teams of four to five people. When Michael asked Dr. Schmidt if they should let the students choose their own teammates so they could work with their friends and make the project more enjoyable, Schmidt quickly corrected Michael's naïve thinking. He was firm: The students should absolutely not form their own teams. He wanted to avoid letting the students make teams that could be easily labeled: the Asian team, the female team, the smart team, the team from Houston, etc. He had learned over decades of teaching that students left to their own devices would self-sort in ways that minimize diversity and maximize comfort and familiarity, aligning by gender, geography, skin color, academic seriousness, or some other element. In other words, the students did not want to get out of their comfort zones. He had also observed that nondiverse teams did not perform as well. Even the "smart team," if fully composed of students who perceived each other to be smarter than average, did not necessarily outperform the others because they suffered from groupthink and lacked some of the creativity and innovation more diverse teams offered.

Instead, the students would submit their first few choices of who they wanted their partners to be and Michael and Dr. Schmidt would sit together and form the teams, looking to put together a mix of backgrounds, which included gender, race, and hometown. This process worked to get better results and also provided a better education for students because they would be exposed to a slightly broader array of people, which could subtly and slowly break down some subconscious biases while pushing them toward higher performance.

The lesson from this example is that managers need to take an active role in forming teams with a range of skills and capabilities. But successful teams in the workplace and community do not need only a mix of skill sets; they also need a mix of viewpoints. The different insights generated from various backgrounds will lead to a better outcome.

But what if the pool of applicants for a team are homogenous? Managers cannot sit back and wait for women or minorities to apply for jobs and then complain if they do not; they must be proactive and get started earlier to fill the pipeline with diverse candidates.

When leaders are faced with the task of filling a vacancy in their company, they often fill it with someone they know directly or indirectly through a trusted source. In that way, they are staying in their comfort zones. Notably, sports team owners are almost exclusively male and white, and historically have hired other white males for key leadership positions. There are some high-profile exceptions that include former players. Michael Jordan is the principal owner of the Charlotte Hornets basketball team and Derek Jeter owns a minority share of the Miami Marlins baseball team and was named the team's CEO. When Johnnie started his professional football career, his first contract was signed by Georgia Frontiere, the first active female majority owner in the NFL.

In the NFL, the intention of diversifying a pool of candidates is captured by the Rooney Rule, which is a requirement that at least one person (in some cases, more than one person) from an underrepresented group be considered for open coaching or senior managerial positions. The Rooney Rule does not require teams to hire women and minorities, but it does require that they are at least considered. Although the rule is not perfect, the thinking behind it is that if women and minorities are never even considered for a position, then they will never be hired. But if teams start to actively interview and scrutinize these candidates in a fair way and if the pool of prospective hires are diverse, then eventually, some positions will be filled by people other than white males.

Over time, that thesis has slowly borne out, as there are more minority coaches and women in leadership positions in the professional sports leagues today than during Johnnie's era in the 1980s. In November 2020, Kim Ng became first woman hired to be a general manager for a baseball team: the Miami Marlins. The same Miami Marlins led by Derek Jeter.

This rule may not be ideal, but it is a step in the right direction because it helps build a network of diverse candidates. That is why career advisors recommend that people expand their networks. In sports, a general manager charged with hiring a head coach often hires one they know and trust in some respect. And when the head coach then hires an offensive or defensive coordinator, they in turn hire a person they know and trust, and the cycle continues. So if the team or company does not have a goal in hiring qualified minorities, and the person hiring does not have any people of color among their network of trusted candidates, then supporting diversity, equity, and inclusion for all becomes more challenging.

We all—not just the billionaire sports team owners—have a role to play in ensuring diversity. At a recent master class for executives that Michael attended, the theme of the day's lesson was gender diversity. Remarkably, the instructor and three panelists were all white males over 50 years old. The panelists, instructor, and the human resources department all could have applied their own version of the NFL Rooney Rule for this masterclass, requiring that at least one of the four lead participants was not a male or white.

Unfortunately, some people will resist a diversification of the workforce. For a company working on gender parity, men might fear they will have to give up their seats to make room for women. That's only true if it is a zero-sum game; but in fact, diversity can lead to growth, which might open up more spots. The phrase "a rising tide lifts all boats" captures this spirit well. And the opposite— inhibited potential for certain groups of people—hurts all of us.

Avoid "Check-box" Diversity

It is also good to avoid a "check-box" approach to diversity. For too many people building teams, they use a checklist. Do we have a woman? Check. Do we have a Latino/a? Check. And so forth. But this approach is shallow and insufficient. The real goal of diversity is to have unique viewpoints, backgrounds, and capabilities.

It's possible to have a team with remarkable racial, ethnic, gender, religious, and geographic diversity, yet every member is a part of the same global class of upwardly mobile, well-educated people. It is possible that at first blush—focusing on outward appearance of skin tone or other parameters such as gender identity or sexual orientation—teams look diverse, yet every member is from a major metropolitan area and is the child of doctors, lawyers, or other professionals. These groups run the risk of having experiences and views of the world that are too similar. Meanwhile, it is also possible for teams that are composed of people with similar skin color to have very different religions, socio-economic upbringings, hometowns, and parents with various education levels. If we focus on the strengths of diversity, which is diversity of backgrounds rather than solely the easily identifiable markers, then we will benefit even more.

As we build teams, we need to ensure something akin to the NFL's Rooney Rule is in effect so we can include candidates of differing backgrounds and perspectives. Supervisors and managers need to be keenly aware of the need for more diversity and include it as a criterion when assessing new team members. And existing team members should advocate for diversifying the team as it expands. Subordinates might not feel comfortable giving recommendations to their bosses, which is why it's critical for the workplace to be one that facilitates open and honest discussion, as described earlier.

A Shared Goal Can Be Used to Build Diverse Teams

This book uses examples from athletics and engineering because those are the stories Johnnie and Michael know from their backgrounds. But the lessons and suggestions put forward are relevant for every sector of society. Athletics is an interesting example of integration because it happened in a very visible way—observers of the integration were highly aware of the addition of nonwhite players to professional rosters—and sports fans were able to see the benefits of diversity, equity, and inclusion unfold right before their eyes. That doesn't mean it was easy or a flawless process though.

When athletes put their uniforms on, they do so to represent their teams in a shared goal of victory. When players compete in their sport, the best ones are more concerned about executing their game plan than they are about the color of their teammate's skin or where they came from.

One of Johnnie's favorite moments during his career took place before the start of each game, when the starting players for each team were introduced to the crowd. They lined up in the tunnel leading to the players' locker room according to their defensive position groups: The big defensive linemen were introduced first, followed by the linebackers, and finally Johnnie's group, the defensive backs. From there, they were introduced one by one, and as their names were called, they would jog out to the 50-yard line where they were greeted by the rest of their teammates. Most of all, Johnnie loved hearing all the different colleges and universities his teammates were from. Their diversity was something the announcer and fans celebrated. Although they were from different parts of the country and of different ethnic groups and backgrounds, when these men entered their huddle to call the play, they knew that their integration would aid them in being successful on the field.

Other institutions are also proponents and beneficiaries of integration for a shared goal. In particular, the U.S. military recruits a wide range of people to share in the mission of improving national security.

Though the military certainly has had its own issues with bias and privilege—for example, generals are still mostly white and male, and there are still barriers for members based on gender identity and sexual orientation —it is designed to serve as a meritocracy. As such, it has been an incredible proving ground for successful and highly visible diverse teams working together for a common goal. This has played out from the Revolutionary War (the first victim at the Boston Massacre, Crispus Attucks, and therefore one of the first Revolutionary War heroes, was a person of color) through the Civil War to both World Wars in the 20th century. While imperfect, the military has been more of a meritocracy than most major institutions. As a result, it has had many collective successes in military operations, as well as individual successes of nonwhites and women who have achieved elevated ranks.

An example is Colin Powell, a retired four-star general who served as the United States' highest-ranking military officer before becoming its first Black Secretary of State from 2001–2005. The military was officially integrated by order of President Harry Truman in 1948. Colin Powell joined the Reserve Officers Training Corp (ROTC) six years after that, then joined the military four years later. A half-century later, he recalled the unique opportunity this way: "By the time I entered the Army in 1958, ten years after the order was signed, the only thing they cared about was could I perform: not whether I was Black, white, poor, rich, West Pointer, or non-West Pointer."[18]

Ultimately, we need to recognize that diversity is a strength that leads to better outcomes, and homogenous teams simply do not perform as well. When more people have an opportunity to achieve their full potential, we all benefit. The examples from athletics and the military show that if we focus on capabilities, outcomes, and merit-based systems for advancement rather than skin color or last names, it is possible to make great progress. In that way, pursuing diverse teams as an input and outcome of diversity, equity, and inclusion benefits all of us.

If diversity isn't happening organically, then it is the responsibility of leaders and other allies to actively pursue it by intention and with forethought, making sure that the team is organized in pursuit of shared goals. And those team members need to bring the uniqueness of their background to the workplace.

CHAPTER 7

Collaborate

As shared in the Harvard Business Review, just making a team more diverse is not enough; the teams also must find a way to work together effectively or they will not reap the benefits of diversity.[19] The researchers go on to note that strong team identity and a sense of top-to-bottom inclusiveness in the organization are critical precon- ditions for success. As Lauren Leader-Chivée wrote in *Crossing the Thinnest Line*, "putting diverse groups together and hoping for a good outcome just through the collision of cultures and ideas rarely works. It takes an entire system of openness, leadership, personal responsibility, accountability, and celebrations of progress."[20]

In other words, building the teams with a mix of backgrounds is a good start, but authentic collaboration is required to make forward progress. To collaborate effectively, we need to recognize the contri- butions each person can make that play to each person's strengths. We cannot pretend that each person has similar math skills or presentation styles, so we also should not pretend we have similar backgrounds. As that same Harvard Business Review piece noted, when teams are formed with people who have different backgrounds and perspectives, team members might want to pretend those differences do not exist to protect group harmony and cohesiveness. But in studies about group behavior, pretending to be colorblind was not as effective as acknowledging racial and ethnic differences. In fact, those differences should be celebrated rather than ignored.

Athletics Can Exemplify Collaborative Diversity

Sports teams routinely promote diversity to achieve their goals. They celebrate each other's differences in speed, strength, or skills. A football team has three core units—offense, defense, and special teams—and each unit has a specific responsibility to provide their team with the best opportunity to win.

The offensive unit is composed of a diverse group of athletes who seeks to score points against a defensive unit equipped with athletes who were carefully selected to prevent the offense from scoring. In similar fashion, the special teams unit is built to compete for kicking plays, such as punts, field goals, and kickoffs. Teamwork is at the center of each unit. All three groups are built to collaborate with each other and give their team the best opportunity to win. If they did not each perform their respective roles in concert and did not trust each other, the team's success would be limited.

Each player has to take responsibility to fulfill the duties of their position and has to rely on their teammates to fulfill their duties. At the same time, they all have to look out for each other and step in to help whenever one player falls down or cannot complete their assignment on their own. For example, if one defensive player cannot tackle the offensive player on his own, other defensive players will help.

Defensive football coaches teach "gang tackling." The best-performing defensive teams are the ones whose individual members work in tandem to prevent the offense from executing sustained drives and scoring points. Johnnie played on one of the best defenses in the history of the University of Texas during his senior year in college. The unit was exceptional in working together consistently via a collaborative effort to perform the defensive plays as planned.

Johnnie's arrival in the NFL was a humbling one. He found himself starting his rookie year in a defensive backfield with three other All-Pros: Nolan Cromwell, Pat Thomas, and Rod Perry. These veterans were considered to be among the best in the NFL at their position, playing on a team that had just played in the Super Bowl. To compound matters, the Rams played an attacking, sophisticated defensive scheme consisting of many different ways to put pressure on the offensive teams they played against.

To assist him in assimilating the defense and to take steps to put himself and the team in the best position for success, Johnnie looked to his veteran defensive teammates for guidance. He learned three things from them, which all summarize what it means to collaborate effectively. The first thing Johnnie learned was to always know if he had help from a teammate in executing the defensive play. This information determined the type of technique Johnnie would utilize on that down. The second thing he learned was that it was critical to always know which teammate would be helping him and where he would be coming from. With this knowledge, Johnnie knew he needed to trust that his teammate would be where he was supposed to be to provide the expected help on the play. The third thing he learned was to know the assignment of all his other teammates on the field for each play. In other words, central to his performance as a top player was the requirement to not only fulfill his own duties but to know everyone else's roles and who would be helping whom and from which direction.

That meant Johnnie had to do a lot of studying to assimilate the aim of the defense on each play. He had to know what each of his 10 teammates were doing on each and every play while also executing his job. This was important because as teammates, they were trusting each other to do their jobs. Together, they were collaborating at a high level, seeking to execute the defensive game plan to put the team in the best position for success.

Each Person Needs to Do Their Part

Although you should be aware of what everyone's job is on the team and be prepared to help, it's important you focus on your job and not worry about your teammate who is doing theirs. Have trust and confidence that they will take care of their business. This lesson is important at critical moments in all aspects of business and life, though it is fairly obvious in the sports world. One such example took place in the 2005 Rose Bowl game between the Michigan Wolverines, coached by legendary coach Lloyd Carr, and the Texas Longhorns, coached by another legend, Mack Brown.

During the game, each team took turns leading the other. Late in the fourth quarter, Michigan kicked a field goal to take a 37–35 lead. Trailing by only two points, all Texas needed was a three-point field goal to win the game. After the Wolverines kicked off to Texas, the offense quickly moved the ball down the field and in field goal range for their kicker Dusty Mangum.

In this way, the Texas quarterback and his offensive unit did their part to give the kicker a chance. With only a few seconds left on the clock, Texas lined up for the field goal attempt, but before they could try, Michigan called a timeout as a strategy to make the kicker nervous.

During the timeout, Coach Brown's field goal team gathered around him. Coach Brown knew the game was riding on this kick, Dusty would feel a lot of pressure, and the team would be nervous. This was a play they had practiced thousands of times during practice and in regular season games, but none were bigger than the one they were about to attempt.

During the timeout, Coach Brown turned to his linemen and reminded them not to worry about Dusty, that he would take care of his job. Coach Brown reminded the linemen to just focus on doing their jobs, which were to provide protection and give Dusty the time he needed to attempt the field goal. If they didn't do their jobs, then Dusty couldn't do his. If they worried about Dusty kicking the ball, then they would fail to give him the time he needed. After the timeout, the field goal team lined up and executed the play as planned, allowing Dusty to make the kick to win the game for the Longhorns, 38–37.

Coach Brown knew that there may be a time when a player may need help, and when he does, he should always be able to rely on a great teammate who will be there to assist. But as this lesson shows, the most important part of being a team player is first making sure we take care of our business as planned. The team is counting on us for that. Only after we take care of our part can we be in position to step in to help our teammates if they are hurt or hindered from being able to perform their jobs. That means if we see a team member at work who is prevented from fully contributing, we need to step up as an ally to give them a voice.

This kind of collaboration is key to all complicated problems. Many of the world's challenges—pandemics, social unrest, poverty, homelessness, unemployment, climate change, national security—are too big for any one person, company, or country to tackle alone. Collaboration across many disciplines, backgrounds, viewpoints, and national boundaries is key.

Climate change is a particularly interesting example because those who must take action (typically Westerners) are culturally and geographically different from the ones who suffer from the inaction (like Bangladeshis, sub-Saharan Africans, and coastal residents). True liberty and justice for all suggests that sometimes, the people who must take action are not the ones who immediately benefit, but they must take action anyway because in the long run, we all benefit from living in a world with lower environmental pollution where everyone is equitably included in society. In a similar vein, we should move toward diversity, equity, and inclusion for all: Members of the existing power structure need to do their part to reinvent their approach and open up so others can join them to the benefit of everyone.

Therefore, just as with a pro football team, without assistance from allies (teammates), meaningful change in the pursuit of liberty and justice for all will be difficult to achieve.

Collaboration Requires Trust

In an article summarizing her research and experience on effective leadership, Jane Wei-Skillern and her co-authors concluded "the single most important factor behind all successful collaborations is trust-based relationships among participants."[21]

If successful collaboration requires trust, how should we build it? There are many classic trust-building exercises, but let us share one with you as an example. It was introduced to us by Daron K. Roberts.

Roberts is an influential thought leader who has charted his own path and defied all stereotypes. After leaving his small hometown, he thrived in a competitive and prestigious honors program at the University of Texas, eventually serving as student body president, which was rare for Black students. After UT, he attended Harvard's Law School and Kennedy School of Government, earning two additional degrees in the process. Though poised for a successful and lucrative legal career, he decided he wanted to be a football coach even though he was never a star player in high school and never played at the collegiate or professional levels. He was undaunted and decided to chase his dream, writing a letter to every single head coach in the NFL and receiving thirty-one rejections in response to his outreach.

But despite all odds, one coach, Herman Edwards of the Kansas City Chiefs, gave him a chance with the caveat that he would have to work for free the first year. Roberts did so, proved his value, and subsequently coached at multiple levels in the NFL and NCAA for several years before deciding to return to academia to teach leadership to students at the University of Texas. His unlikely success through an unconventional path while overcoming biases along the way is an inspirational tale captured in his autobiography *Call an Audible*[22].

Roberts also authored a successful children's book titled *A Kid's Book About Empathy*, which captures some of the lessons on empathy he teaches his five kids and his hundreds of students each year. He works with student athletes and honors students from all walks of life at the university, and as part of his teaching routine, he helps encourage a sense of team by teaching empathy. Empathy is a key ingredient for the goals and themes in this book. It's especially useful for building trust.

To teach empathy, Roberts uses a classic exercise, dividing his class into pairs and being proactive about assigning unlikely partners together rather than letting the students self-select. The students take turns wearing a blindfold while their partners guide them long distances across campus. One lesson this exercise reveals is that race, religion, ethnicity, and gender become less important when you are depending on someone else to guide you to your destination.[23] Unstated is that the blindfold makes it so the other person's skin color cannot be seen and is irrelevant. Navigating safely from one location to another without getting hurt requires trust by the blindfolded partner and is an allegory for what is necessary for successful teams. Team members have to be there to help each other, but they also have to trust that each person will do their part. If a member of a sports team feels the need to play his or her own position *and* every other person's position, the player will become exhausted and the team will surely fail. Successful teams expect every person to fulfill their role while each stands ready to step up in case they can't complete their task.

Trust and empathy can go hand in hand when promoting overall team success. Therefore it is in everyone's best interest to remove our focus on race, gender, or other outward indicators so we can instead focus on our common objective—whether that is to walk safely across campus or some other higher goal. For Roberts' exercise, a blindfold was a useful tool to turn off our perception of skin color and instead listen to the essence of what the guide was sharing. It is also reminiscent of the blindfolded Lady Justice, who holds a balance and is often positioned outside of courthouses. The blindfolded statue sends a few important messages about the moral authority of law that is applied in a jurisprudent way. The balance indicates that legal proceedings and the law should be applied fairly based on the facts that are presented, not tilting in favor of one person or group over another. The blindfold signifies impartiality, indicating that justice should be applied without regard to wealth, status, power, or skin color. That is, the jurors or judges should not look to see who the person in question is but should instead only listen to the facts of the situation, giving rise to the pithy maxim, "Justice is blind."

In that way, Roberts' blindfold exercise and the blindfolded Lady Justice share the same meaning: Don't get distracted by what a person looks like. Focus on the important facts of the situation. If a student without a blindfold is guiding a student with a blindfold and says to step to the left to avoid hitting a tree, the interpretation of that guidance should not vary based on the skin color of the guide. As we apply that lesson to our teams, that does not mean we should be colorblind. Rather, we should use the essential facts of each person's essence instead of their outward appearance. To maintain that trust within organizations, McKinsey & Company concluded in their research that it is critical for organizations to use fair and equitable standards along with a level playing field to consider promotions, mete out punishments, or fill positions.[24] Offering special treatment for one group or another will rapidly diminish trust and undermine successful collaboration.

Although not perfect, the intent of pro sports' systems to select candidates for their team are designed to provide a fair and equitable playing field for participants. Their goal is to find the best candidate for the job and fill their roster with the finest group of athletes that will give them the best opportunity to win. Part of the evaluation process takes place between white lines, where candidates are competing with a clear set of rules and guidelines. What is ironic is that within this limited framework to create a level playing field, pro sports has become a leader when it comes to diversity, equity, and inclusion for the athletes competing in their respective sport. However, even though significant strides have been made on the field or court, we still need allies in key roles and places to continue to make social progress in the coaching ranks, front office, and other areas in society.

Allies and Champions Are Important

Returning to the relay race example earlier, everyone has to do their part for a successful race. But it's not just the runners who contribute; it's also the coaches, trainers, nutritionists, and other supportive staff.

Critically, because the existing power structure is dominated by white males, they have an important opportunity to serve as allies.

In *Crossing the Thinnest Line*, Leader-Chivée clarifies this point, writing, "The truth is for our nation to fully profit from diversity, we need many, many more Americans—to be blunt, especially straight white men—to lead the charge."[25] She goes on to note, however, that the entire burden of solving society's problems with inclusivity do not rest with the majority, so we all have a role to play to bridge divides. The way she terms it, although white males do not satisfy any diversity check-boxes, they can in fact develop a sense of acquired diversity— that is, a more global and open-minded viewpoint about the value of different perspectives—and then use their positions of influence to push for change. Returning to an example from earlier, women could not grant themselves the right to vote since they were not in political office. They needed white male allies and champions to admit them into the power structure.

There have been many white male champions in the past: Benjamin Franklin was an active abolitionist at the state level; President Abraham Lincoln emancipated slaves nationwide; President Harry Truman integrated the U.S. military; and President Lyndon Johnson was a powerful force in support of civil rights. Those champions were vitally important. They did not work alone of course, and they could not have achieved their work without the help of others, but they were key members of the team. Such is the way it will be within most communities and organizations.

In summary, collaboration means we all have a role to play. We must rely on each other to fulfill our own roles, trust that each will do what is expected of their position and be ready to step in to help when a teammate cannot meet their responsibilities. These different positions on the team include people who are currently marginalized, those who can influence those in power, and the champions and allies in the power structure who themselves are not diverse but can acquire diversity in advance of the cause toward a more inclusive society.

CHAPTER 8

Align Actions With Goals and Values

When we set a goal and head out to achieve it, we naturally encounter twists, turns, obstacles, or barriers along the way, but we cannot let those obstacles stop us from making forward progress. One of the challenges we can face during our journey occurs when actions are in conflict with our personal values. These kinds of conflicting situations are oftentimes distressing, but what if it's not our bosses, colleagues, or neighbors who create those conflicts? What if it's our own actions that are not aligned?

Unfortunately, too many of us have not taken the time to identify our core values. Even fewer take the time to make sure they are living by those values. Values reflect the principles that are important to us regarding our family, society, an entity, a team, or an individual. In business, stated values serve as guidelines for making policy decisions and setting priorities. For individuals, they serve as criteria for making life decisions, such as choosing a partner or a career path. Values define the character and personality of the entity or the individual. They also provide constraints and guidance for actions.

Achieving success in any endeavor requires action, which must align with the person's goals and values. While determining a goal can be a difficult hurdle for most people, determining the goal alone isn't enough. Action must be consistently taken over a period of time, often while encountering roadblocks that can potentially hinder progress.

Improvement Is a Continuous Process

Aesop's fable of *The Tortoise and the Hare* teaches that "slow and steady wins the race." The hare, who is much faster than the tortoise but applies intermittent effort and stops for frequent breaks, ultimately loses a race to the slow-moving tortoise, who, step by step, grinds away to move toward the destination without hesitation. That kind of determination will be necessary for achieving diversity, equity, and inclusion for all. We will have to apply steady effort to achieve these goals.

Along the way, it's important to ensure our steps align with our goals and values. Steps that take us in the wrong direction—that is, steps that are not aligned with our goals—inhibit our progress. There are many pathways to a destination, but the pathways that align with our values for integrity, decency, honesty, and empathy must be top priority. This requires us to check our biases and blind spots. Even the people who aim to support diversity, equity, and inclusion for all do not always behave in supportive ways. In these situations, beliefs, habits, attitudes, and expectations are not properly aligned with desired outcomes.

Sustained improvement does not happen from effort that is exerted only once. It is a continuous process, so those committed to achieving their goals can never stop working on them. While "slow and steady wins the race" is a useful explanation for the proper approach, perhaps a friendly amendment to that concept is the idea that "the race is never over." As we make progress toward achieving our goals, we need to continue to elevate them. One companywide meeting on sensitive subjects like diversity is not sufficient; it needs to be followed by structural changes, such as improved hiring practices, mentoring, a more trustworthy work environment, and so on.

In the world of athletics, the game is all about improving every day. Professional athletes practice the fundamentals of their sport on a daily basis, regardless of what occurred the day before. No coach will take their team through just one practice and expect them to be successful. For them, success is a daily process of incremental action steps, not a destination. Therefore, no matter what level of success or number of setbacks they experience as a professional athlete, they know the most important next step is practice. Success is bred from the continuous process of identifying and successfully practicing the fundamentals of their profession.

In football, there are three fundamentals at the center of the game: blocking, tackling, and protecting the football. The team that most consistently practices these three fundamentals usually wins the game. Hall of Fame players and legends of a sport are those who successfully practice the fundamentals of their profession against the world's greatest competition, often in a hostile environment. These are athletes of all physical sizes, from all walks of life, and from many different ethnic groups. For a professor, the fundamentals are teaching, reviewing, and writing scholarly work. The most prolific professors write every day.

What are the lessons learned from this process in the sports world? Let's begin with the understanding that no player will become a Hall of Famer or legend in their sport just because they are a supreme athlete. Athleticism is a critical ingredient, but talent isn't enough; they also need problem-solving to consistently perform the fundamentals of their profession to the best of their ability despite adverse circumstances. Both coaches and players are keenly aware of this. Three quotes from three elite leaders in their profession capture this point.

Bill Belichick, the longtime head coach of the New England Patriots football team and all-time leader in Super Bowl wins, is one of the most consistent and successful head coaches in the history of the NFL. Coach Belichick is famous for stating, "Dependability is more important than ability." When he makes this point, he is referring to the expectation he holds that his entire organization, from management to scouting to coaches to players, will be dependable and consistent in solving problems and practicing the core elements of their jobs. Natural ability is desirable of course, but without a reliable application of that ability, progress is not assured. Lesson learned: Be dependable in practicing the fundamentals of your profession.

Sean McVay was the youngest head coach in the history of the NFL when he led his team, the Los Angeles Rams, to the Super Bowl. Coach McVay likes to say, "The standard is the standard." He is referring to the expectations he has for his entire organization, not just the marquee players: Everyone has to meet a high, objective standard. The standard is not lowered or raised for anyone, which creates a context where every player is treated fairly and equitably. This is the way it should be in all work settings. Both bosses and employees need to be treated with the same set of consistent, clear standards. Creating expectations that vary breeds inequities and undermines morale, ultimately compromising individual potential and reducing overall team performance. Lesson learned: Maintain the standard associated with practicing the fundamentals of your profession.

Marquise Goodwin, former Olympic long jumper and NFL wide receiver, often says, "Consistency is more important than perfection." He is referring to all of us in society. If we are consistent, we can fine-tune our performance. But if our actions vary widely from day to day with no rhyme or reason, improvement will remain elusive. Lesson learned: Do not allow waiting for the perfect time or situation to prevent you from consistently practicing the fundamentals of your profession.

Consistent effort in the fundamentals is key to continuous improvement. It is also one of the common ingredients of success across careers. Becoming elite requires focused and consistent improvement. In her book *Why Are All the Black Kids Sitting Together in the Cafeteria?*, Beverly Daniel Tatum notes that people who have an effort mindset rather than an ability mindset are more likely to succeed.[26] This is especially true in academia.

Professors hold privileged positions in society. Tenured professorships are one of the rare careers—along with some lifetime judgeships—that are protected, which means those who occupy the position cannot be removed from their position except in extreme cases. The privilege of this situation is intended to give independence so professors and judges can speak publicly and decide what they think is best without fear of losing their jobs. With this independence comes a responsibility to serve society. Professors serve through teaching and research, and judges make decisions through impartial jurisprudence, basing their judgment purely on the facts and evidence.

In Michael's view, being a professor is the best job in the world. It holds a respected position in the community, is a liberated way to live, and offers great longevity. It is not unusual for professors to be productive scholars well into their 80s. In fact, one of his faculty colleagues in the mechanical engineering department at the University of Texas at Austin, John Goodenough, consistently showed up to work well into his 90s. Michael and Dr. Goodenough would often have lunch together at the local greasy burger spot along with faculty colleagues. Dr. Goodenough taught into his early 90s and supervised researchers and published papers into his mid- to late 90s. In fact, he often remarked that he had his most productive year ever in his mid-90s. In 2019, at the age of 98, he became the world's oldest Nobel Laureate, receiving the Nobel Prize in Chemistry for his invention of the lithium-ion battery that makes portable electronics and electric vehicles competitive and popular because of their small weight and size.

A professorship is a distinguished and desirable position that is very difficult to achieve. A typical faculty opening at a major university will receive hundreds of applications, usually from the brightest students at Ph.D. programs worldwide, which are themselves composed of the brightest undergraduate students before that. But this distinguished, privileged position also comes with the burdens of a high workload and obligations to faculty colleagues, dozens to hundreds of students each semester, professional peers, and so forth. Dr. Goodenough kept honing his craft all the way into his late 90s, and that is what it takes to become elite. Michael has been known to say that if professors only work five days a week, they aren't showing their job enough respect, but if professors work seven days a week, they aren't showing their friends and families enough respect. Johnnie's observations of athletics are similar. Becoming an elite athlete requires continuous improvement, but even the world's very best athletes have at least one day of rest each week.

In addition to working on his craft, Michael also builds fitness goals into his daily regimen, aiming to walk at least two hours every day. These walks can be used for phone calls, to flesh out books with co-authors as Johnnie and Michael have done, or to facilitate clear thinking, which is a critical component of professorial work. Whether it's raining or cold, Michael aims to take this walk. Johnnie has a similar approach; however, fitness is already part of his athletic regimen, so unlike Michael, he does not need to add it in. Instead, Johnnie adds in the academic components of reading and writing that otherwise would be missing from his daily routine.

Why would they do this? Because fitness and physical health are coupled with mental health and peace of mind. By building these elements into their daily routine, they make progress on both their professional and personal goals. Consistent daily routines are a great thing; however, the bigger the goal, the more likely we will encounter obstacles, barriers, or setbacks along the way. The key is in how we handle them when they appear. This is where we can take a closer look at how we naturally respond when our expectations are not met, and the role our life experiences, beliefs, habits, attitudes, and expectations play in the process of aligning our actions with our goals and values.

When Johnnie looked back on why he struggled in math before taking Mrs. Mayer's algebra class, it was in part because of what he perceived as negative experiences in previous math classes. He had not performed according to his teachers' expectations. He was told by others that he was not a good math student, and as a result, he often felt discouraged and helpless. Although there may have been several factors contributing to why he failed to perform well in the subject, including poor study habits, his fears came from many of his prior experiences and the comments he had heard from others, and he locked on to them. When he did, he locked out the possibilities and opportunities to excel based on his true potential.

Mrs. Mayer helped change his beliefs, habits, and expectations surrounding the subject while properly aligning his actions with his goals and values in the class—a process with which he was very famil-iar, because he was being taught the same thing in football. Johnnie and his teammates were trained to *lock on and lock out*. Coaches instruct players to *lock on* to the things they have control of, like the fundamen-tals of the game, and *lock out* those things that are out of their control, such as the crowd noise if they are playing a road game in front of a hostile crowd or the conditions if they are playing in really bad weather.

Locking on to actions that align with your goals and locking out of distractions or actions that don't align will enable swifter progress.

We recommend everyone take the time to identify their core values and articulate them. From our decades of mentoring and leadership, we have found that too few people take this step. As a consequence, their life choices are based on habit, tradition, or other people's expectations rather than their own decisions about how they would like to behave or what they would like to achieve. We hope you will consider the importance of a harmonious society through diversity, equity, and inclusion as part of your values.

In addition, it is hard to know whether you are moving in alignment with or in opposition to your values if you don't know what they are in the first place. Once you've identified and articulated those values, it's a matter of applying steady pressure. While simply writing your values down on a piece of paper is a nice start, it is not sufficient. You must strive to make daily progress. It is never too late to learn, it is never too late to improve, and as demonstrated by Dr. Goodenough, if we are healthy then each of us can keep making societal contributions well into our 90s if we so choose.

This journey is difficult and never-ending and can be frustrating and challenging. But it can also be rewarding. Perhaps you will take that first step, then pass along the lessons you've learned to those around you. If you do, we will all be able to work together to make this world a better place for all of us.

Epilogue

We Followed These Eight Steps

It's worth noting that Michael and Johnnie followed these eight steps to write this book. In their view, these eight steps are universally helpful for building relationships regardless of profession or personal description. They were both already aware of step one—that progress starts with each of them—as that had been central to their coaching and mentoring for decades. That step is what pushed them to develop their thoughts and write them down in the first place.

Acting in the spirit of brotherhood—that is, loving your neighbor—was also necessary. In this case, the neighborhood is the book, and they as the authors were the neighbors. They had to recognize that they each belong in this neighborhood and deserve proper treatment from the other. Collaborative projects can be difficult because each team member might have a different approach. Treating each other as they wished to be treated was important to facilitate a harmonious collaboration. This is especially true because writing is a vulnerable process (and even more so about a sensitive topic like diversity, equity and inclusion for all). Putting thoughts and feelings on paper exposes the author to the risk of criticism and scrutiny. Most people are afraid to share their personal writings with others, yet Johnnie and Michael had to do that frequently as the first critic for their work was always each other. That means their reviews, edits, and suggestions had to come from a pursuit of a shared purpose and a place of respect for each other rather than an "us versus them" mentality.

Johnnie and Michael have different writing styles, habits, and approaches, so it took a lot of patience and respect to integrate their voices successfully without declaring whose voice gets to be in the neighborhood.

They also had to talk things through. Much of this book was fleshed out by near-daily one- to two-hour phone calls during the first month they wrote. These discussions would be used to address tone, scope, approach, audience, intent, principles, and so forth. Before they ever put pen to paper, they talked about the book at length, and that helped them sort out any issues before they became bigger challenges down the road.

In addition, both authors had to expand their comfort zones. When Michael told his students he was writing this book, he revealed he had never been so professionally terrified in his life. The students were surprised since he was already a published author of multiple books and had tackled difficult topics such as climate change in public forums for many years. The reason for fear was because he was out of his comfort zone. Decades of training in engineering, innovation, energy, and the environment gave him a great sense of confidence on those topics, but dealing with society's inequities felt like wholly new ground and a place with little intellectual footing for him. The students were very supportive, thinking he usually had something smart to say, which at first made the situation worse. Michael didn't feel like he had anything smart to say, and he was worried about failing spectacularly in a very public way and letting his students down. But he had to press forward and overcome his fears of missteps or backlash. Ultimately, their encouragement helped a lot. They and other mentors were excellent champions for him.

Johnnie also had to expand his comfort zone. Though he had also authored multiple books, it was intimidating to have a professor check his work and mark up his drafts. Michael's editing style can be rough and exposing himself to such criticism on a routine basis aroused fears and insecurities. Together, they aimed to model how people can live with discomfort and risk exposing themselves to share their journey.

To tackle this project effectively, they had to be open with their biases and blind spots. Michael's background as a white son of a professor in an urban environment is mostly one of privilege. That does not mean it was devoid of hard work or setbacks, but it does mean there were advantages that worked to his benefit, not because of anything he did in particular but because of his identification as a member of a particular group. Johnnie's background as one of 11 children in a Black, rural household on the welfare system was much different. Though he also had some privileges as a result of his athleticism, his path through life required him to endure many unfair practices that worked against him.

Those experiences and the context of their upbringings present them with different biases and blind spots that are hard for them to identify and correct. Being honest with themselves about these is an important step in the movement toward diversity, equity, and inclusion, and they had to bring that honesty to their writing. They also had to give each other feedback about specific word choices, tone, and possible misinterpretations.

Just as they recommend for readers and organizations, they had to build a diverse team to complete this project. Johnnie and Michael are different in many ways: Black and white, rural and urban, athletic and intellectual, baby boomer and Generation X, and so forth. But there are more elements of diversity that were missing from their viewpoints, so they expanded their team to include a foreword author, an editor, proofreader, reviewers, and mentors who brought other dimensions of diversity to the project.

Then, they had to collaborate. They collaborated on every aspect of this book: the cover art, the scope, the writing, the editing, and more. Every aspect of this book was discussed and worked on by both of them. The goal—with the exception of the foreword and prologues—was to create one voice and an integrated set of recommendations. They hope you can do the same.

In addition, they also had to serve as allies and champions for each other. Johnnie is giving Michael a chance to be a part of the dialogue with more compassion and understanding, and Michael is giving Johnnie a chance to tell his story with an author who brings credibility from different sectors. Members of the entrenched power structure should absolutely be an ally right now.

Critically, Johnnie and Michael's actions had to be aligned with their goals and values. The goal is to support diversity, equity, and inclusion for all, so they had to take action in a way that was consistent with their values. Working on this book became a daily exercise to make steady progress with their writing by having conversations with others, reading, and engaging with other stakeholders. There were many other actions they could have taken—silence or continuing with their lives business as usual, for example—but those options are not helpful for the authors' journey.

Ethics and Dignity Need to Be at the Core of Our Actions

Johnnie and Michael's values often guide how they treat people and the decisions they make daily. Usually, culture, background, or life experiences contribute to the biases we hold and the way we view the world. Understanding that we all have biases and the role they play in our lives is why the idea of ethics and dignity runs through the core of the eight ways to support diversity, equity, and inclusion for all. Treating everyone with dignity and applying high ethical standards to our engagements with others benefits our individual situations while helping to elevate those around us. These core concepts will be helpful not just for justice but for other issues we might care about, including our careers, our families, and our peace of mind.

A tidbit of wisdom can be shared through the following riddle. Q: When is the best time to plant a tree? A: Twenty years ago. Big strong trees that provide beauty, shade, lumber, and food do not grow overnight: They grow over decades. Similarly, an ethical reputation and authentic, long-lasting relationships based on trust cannot be built overnight: They are formed from steady effort over years.

Johnnie and Michael recommend that you lead a principle-centered life. Identify your values, make sure dignity and ethics are central to them, then take consistent action to live by them. The authors think this is a crucial aspect of working toward a society that is diverse, equitable, and inclusive for all. If a white engineer and Black athlete can come together and find such similarities, then so can the world. We should all do our part and reading this book is just the start.

Acknowledgments

Like any project, this book came into existence because of a large team of people who made direct and indirect contributions to its completion. We would like to thank them and acknowledge their contributions.

Lyric Dodson's editing was invaluable. She is an insightful reader who has expertise on issues related to diversity, equity, and inclusion, so we recommend her for other authors who need an editor or sensitivity reader. Megan Sever provided excellent proofreading and copyediting. You shouldn't judge a book by its cover, but we are thankful nevertheless for Jeff Phillips, who helped us bring the book to life with a clean, simple look and feel. We appreciate Teresa Palacios Smith who agreed to leave her comfort zone to author the foreword. Our reviewers Allison Schnettler, Daron K. Roberts, Tricia Berry, John Tortora, Eric Impraim, Bobbi Burke, Rebecca Neal, and Gino Blefari gave us timely and constructive criticism that kept us on track, and for that, we are thankful.

We also want to thank our wives, Julie and Julia, for their patience and encouragement. We could not have written this book without their support. We would also like to thank our children Kirk, Collin, Camille, Evelyn, David, and Maverick.

Johnnie would like to acknowledge his good friend and mentor Gino Blefari again, who in addition to serving as a reviewer, is one of the most committed CEOs to supporting diversity, equity, and inclusion for all in society. Johnnie would also like to acknowledge all of his former teammates at La Grange High School, the University of Texas at Austin, Los Angeles Rams, and Seattle Seahawks. Last but certainly not least, Johnnie would like to thank Michael for his willingness to step out of his comfort zone and play such a huge role in bringing the mission and vision of this book to life. He epitomizes the definition of a loyal and dedicated teammate, and he brings true meaning to the word "collaboration."

Michael would like to acknowledge Tricia Berry again, who in addition to serving as a reviewer, also taught Michael many useful lessons through the faculty diversity trainings she orchestrated. Michael also gained important insights about building diverse teams, Imposter Syndrome, and working into our nineties from his faculty colleague mentors in mechanical engineering, Nobel Laureate John Goodenough and Professors Phil Schmidt and Jack Howell.

Selection for the Presidential Leadership Scholars program organized by Presidents George W. Bush and William J. Clinton was a once-in-a-lifetime leadership training opportunity for Michael. He very much appreciates the time the presidents and their staffs spent with him and other members of his training cohort. The lessons they taught weave their way through this book. In particular, Professor Mike Hemphill's training on how to think, collaborate, and communicate was life changing.

Michael would also like to thank Johnnie, as the idea for collaborating on the book was originally his, and thankfully, he did not give up when Michael refused on multiple occasions to participate. His patience and persistence are appreciated, and Michael could not ask for a better collaborator for this project.

About the Authors

Johnnie Johnson serves as president and CEO of World Class Coaches, one of the world's premier personal, professional, and executive coaching companies. He is a well-known author, inspirational speaker, executive peak performance coach, and entrepreneur. He spent nine years in real estate sales, where he produced more than a hundred transactions a year as a top-producing real estate agent.

Johnnie is the author of the popular book *You're Closer Than You Think Whether You Realize It or Not*. He founded the Moving Families Initiative, a comprehensive resource for helping families move, and created the Moving Families Foundation, a nonprofit that assists young children and high school students in managing the physical and emotional challenges of changing neighborhoods, schools, and friends when they move or relocate.

As the team's number one draft pick, Johnnie excelled for 10 years in the NFL as an All-Pro safety for the Los Angeles Rams. At the University of Texas at Austin, he was a two-time consensus All-American in football. The Downtown Athletic Club of New York City, the entity that awards the Heisman Trophy, named him the Most Outstanding Defensive Back in the United States. In 2007, Johnnie was elected to the National Football Foundation & College Football Hall of Fame.

Michael E. Webber is based in Austin, Texas and Paris, France, where he serves as the chief science and technology officer at ENGIE, a global energy and infrastructure services company. Webber is also the Josey Centennial Professor in Energy Resources at the University of Texas at Austin. Webber's expertise spans research and education at the convergence of engineering, policy, and commercialization on topics related to innovation, energy, and the environment. His book *Power Trip: The Story of Energy* was the basis of an eponymous six-part documentary series on PBS. Michael was selected as a member of the fourth class of the Presidential Leadership Scholars, which is a leadership training program organized by Presidents George W. Bush and Bill Clinton.

Michael has authored more than 400 publications and holds six patents. He holds a B.S. and B.A. from the University of Texas at Austin and an M.S. and Ph.D. in mechanical engineering from Stanford University.

Endnotes

1   Robin DiAngelo, *White Fragility: Why It's So Hard for White People to Talk About Racism*, Beacon Press (2018).

2   Rushworth M. Kidder, *How Good People Make Tough Choices: Resolving the Dilemmas of Ethical Living*, Harper, New York (2009).

3   Simon Blackburn, *Ethics: A Very Short Introduction*. Oxford: Oxford University Press, (2003).

4   Rose Cahalan, "Star Power,"*Alcalde* March/April 2012. https://alcalde.texasexes.org/2012/02/star-power/ [accessed September 6, 2020].

5   Nancy H. Welsh, "Racially Restrictive Covenants in the United States: A Call to Action," *Agora Journal of Urban Planning and Design*, 130-142 (2018).

6   Margot Lee Shetterly, *Hidden Figures: The American Dream and the Untold Story of the Black Women Mathematicians Who Helped Win the Space Race*, William Morrow and Company (2017).

7   Beverly Daniel Tatum, *Why Are All the Black Kids Sitting Together in the Cafeteria? And Other Conversations About Race*, Basic Books (2017).

8   Elie Wiesel, The Nobel Acceptance Speech delivered in Oslo, Norway, December 10, 1986. https://eliewieselfoundation.org/elie-wiesel/nobelprizespeech/ [Accessed November 23, 2020]

9   Epictetus Quotes, BrainyQuote.com, BrainyMedia Inc, 2020. https://www.brainyquote.com/quotes/epictetus_106298 , accessed November 23, 2020

10   Cameron Yarbrough, Tweeted by @yarbroughcam, September 4, 2020: https://twitter.com/yarbroughcam/status/1301913412478201858 [Accessed November 23, 2020]

11   Cameron Yarbrough, Tweeted by @yarbroughcam, September 4, 2020: https://twitter.com/yarbroughcam/status/1301984836505141249 [Accessed November 23, 2020]

12   Lauren Leader-Chivée, *Crossing the Thinnest Line*, Center Street, New York, 2016.

13   Sundiatu Dixon-Fyle, Kevin Dolan, Vivian Hunt and Sar Prince, "Diversity wins: How inclusion matters," *McKinsey & Company*, May 19, 2020. https://www.mckinsey.com/featured-insights/diversity-and-inclusion/diversity-wins-how-inclusion-matters# [Accessed 10 Oct 2020].

14   David Rock and Heidi Grant, "Why Diverse Teams Are Smarter," *Harvard Business Review*, November 4, 2016.

15   "HP Computers are Racist," YouTube video posted December 10, 2009. https://www.youtube.com/watch?v=t4DT3tQqgRM [Accessed November 23, 2020]

16   Mallory Simon, "HP looking into claim webcams can't see black people,"CNN, December 23, 2009. https://www.cnn.com/2009/TECH/12/22/hp.webcams/ [Accessed November 23, 2020]

17   Laszlo Bock and Brian Welle, Ph.D, "You don't know what you don't know: How our unconscious minds undermine the workplace," Official Google Blog, September 25, 2014. https://googleblog.blogspot.com/2014/09/you-dont-know-what-you-dont-know-how.html [Accessed November 23, 2020]

18   Jim Garamone, "Former Chairman Discusses Truman's 1948 Integration Order," *American Forces Press Service*, July 28, 2008.

19   David Rock, Heidi Grant, and Jacqui Grey, "Diverse Teams Feel Less Comfortable – and That's Why They Perform Better," *Harvard Business Review*, September 22, 2016. https://hbr.org/2016/09/diverse-teams-feel-less-comfortable-and-thats-why-they-perform-better [Accessed 10 October 2020].

20   Lauren Leader-Chivée, *Crossing the Thinnest Line*, Center Street, New York, 2016.

21   Jane Wei-Skillern, David Ehrlichman, and David Sawyer, "The Most Impactful Leaders You Have Never Heard Of," *Stanford Social Innovation Review*, September 16, 2015.

22   Daron K. Roberts, *Call an Audible: Let My Pivot from Harvard Law to NFL Coach Inspire Your Transition*, River Grove Books (2017).

23   Danielle Lopez, "In Their Shoes," *Alcalde*, September/October 2020.

24 "Diversity wins: How inclusion matters," McKinsey & Company, May 19, 2020. https://www.mckinsey.com/featured-insights/diversity-and-inclusion/diversity-wins-how-inclusion-matters# [Accessed 10 Oct 2020].

25 Lauren Leader-Chivée, *Crossing the Thinnest Line*, Center Street, New York, 2016.

26 Beverly Daniel Tatum, *Why Are All the Black Kids Sitting Together in the Cafeteria? And Other Conversations About Race*, Basic Books (2017).